WITHDRAWN

SCIENCE FICTION

This is a volume in the
Arno Press collection

SCIENCE FICTION

ADVISORY EDITORS

R. Reginald

Douglas Menville

See last pages of this volume
for a complete list of titles

LINGUISTICS AND LANGUAGES
IN SCIENCE FICTION-FANTASY

MYRA EDWARDS BARNES

ARNO PRESS
A New York Times Company
New York — 1975

Reprint Edition 1974 by Arno Press Inc.

Copyright © 1971 by Myra Edwards Barnes

Reprinted by permission of Myra Edwards Barnes

SCIENCE FICTION
ISBN for complete set: 0-405-06270-2
See last pages of this volume for titles.

Manufactured in the United States of America

Library of Congress Cataloging in Publication Data

Barnes, Myra Jean.
    Linguistics and languages in science fiction-fantasy.

    (Science fiction)
    Originally presented as the author's thesis, East Texas State University, 1971.
    1. Science fiction, American--History and criticism.
2. Fantastic fiction, English--History and criticism.
3. Imaginary languages in literature. 4. Linguistics.
I. Title. II. Series.
PS374.S35B3 1974   823'.0876   74-17864
ISBN 0-405-06319-9

LINGUISTICS AND LANGUAGES IN SCIENCE FICTION-FANTASY

by

MYRA EDWARDS BARNES

Submitted to the Faculty of the Graduate School of
East Texas State University
in partial fulfillment of the requirements
for the degree of
DOCTOR OF PHILOSOPHY
August, 1971

Copyright 1971 by Myra Edwards Barnes

ABSTRACT

LINGUISTICS AND LANGUAGES IN SCIENCE FICTION-FANTASY

Myra Edwards Barnes, Ph.D.
East Texas State University, 1971

Advisor: Fred A. Tarpley

Purpose of the Study: Modern science fiction and fantasy is a literature of communication. Because language is the most common medium of communication, one purpose of this study was to select imaginary, fictional languages created within works of science fiction-fantasy for the fictional characters to speak and to examine the basic features of the imaginary languages, using criteria of linguistic principles, to test the hypothetical speakability or linguistic verisimilitude of the created languages. Another purpose was to ascertain the extent to which linguistics, as a descriptive science, appears as a literary device in utopian and anti-utopian fiction, now most prominent in science fiction form. A third purpose was to propose more versatile uses of linguistics as a tool in literary criticism. Among the primary authors are Isaac Asimov, Jack Vance, Sprague de Camp, Robert Nathan, Robert Graves, and J. R. R. Tolkien.

Procedure: Isolating specific areas of specialization within the field of linguistics--historical linguistics, language transcription, semantics, anthropological linguistics, artificial and basic language creation, and aspects of language and culture--the principles in that area were used to form a criteria by which the imaginary languages could be measured. Some fictional selections contained a language system sufficiently developed to allow testing for its feasibility as a hypothetically speakable language, and others contained various aspects of language that illustrate the use of actual linguistic principles as a major literary device. In some instances, the imaginary language was developed and utilized in such a way that only by linguistic analysis could the work gain value in literary criticism.

Findings: Among approximately thirty selections examined for this study, not one was found to contain meaningless gibberish that was purported to be a language. Although authors did not always explain the rules upon which the imaginary languages were constructed, it was often possible to analyze the grammatical structure of the language as it was illustrated in conversation throughout the book. Several selections contained a surprisingly complex, thorough, and speakable language system. In other selections, the theme of fantasy allowed authors to construct a hypothetical history for the English language, illustrating how the events of history could have produced a much-changed English language, and how the hypothetical future history of the world could influence the future of the English language; the criteria of actual historical linguistics indicated the plausibility of such languages developing from their hypothetical history, and only such linguistic analysis could discern the scholarship with which each author developed his theme.

It was found that technical terminology rarely appears in the creation or illustration of a fictional language, although personal correspondence with several primary authors indicates that the authors have purposely avoided technical linguistic terms. It was found that writers in this genre are becoming increasingly concerned with the serious prospect of establishing a means of communication with beings from other planets whose physiology and language-producing organs might differ greatly from any known today. Speculative linguistics, as it is illustrated in science fiction, is firmly based on present knowledge in the field of descriptive linguistics, and no part of any selection contained within this study was found to violate any fact of modern linguistic knowledge.

Conclusion: Because the most recent literary selections are concerned with vocal communication more often than older works of science fiction, it is apparent that linguistics and language are becoming increasingly important in speculative literature. Although writers utilize these literary aspects in their stories, there is a definite lack of linguistic terminology; the general reading public could be educated into the science of linguistics as it already has been into the physical sciences. The growth of science fiction and fantasy as a literary genre may prove traditional methods of literary criticism inadequate; in such a case, this "literature of communication" may profit by an application of the "science of communication"--linguistics--in literary criticism.

ACKNOWLEDGMENTS

I cannot thank many of the people who helped in the initial stages of this study; I never learned their names. They were people who "read something like that one time," and, fortunately, were able to remember the titles of some of the primary works that are included in this study. I am grateful to several authors who provided personal comments on their writings, as well as suggestions for their own criticism. And I am especially indebted to Hal Hall, both a librarian and a long-time science fiction fan, who devoted many hours of personal research for my benefit in the resource center for science fiction literature, a part of the Texas A&M University library.

For reasons that have extended beyond routine duty, I owe a special debt to Dr. Fred Tarpley.

But most of all, I wish to acknowledge Berry, Brandon, and Jolie--my husband, son, and daughter--who have acted with patience and encouragement throughout a tedious period of composition, and for whom this work was first begun.

TABLE OF CONTENTS

PREFACE i

Chapter

    I. INTRODUCTION 1
   II. GROWTH OF LINGUISTIC REALISM IN FICTION 14
  III. LINGUISTIC NOVELTIES AND MODERN FICTION 30
   IV. HISTORICAL LINGUISTICS AND HYPOTHETICAL HISTORY . 45
    V. SPEAKING THE SAME LANGUAGE 64
   VI. LEXICOGRAPHY AND "DOCTORED DICTIONARIES" 82
  VII. HOW TO LEARN MARTIAN 97
 VIII. WHAT PEOPLE MEAN AND HOW CARROTS SAY IT 114
   IX. THE LANGUAGE OF THOUGHT CONTROL 140

CONCLUSION 171
BIBLIOGRAPHY 181
APPENDIX 191

PREFACE

This is a study in applying the principles of modern linguistics as a measurement of modern fiction, but only to a specific issue that appears in a specific type of fiction that was never intended to be measured in quite this way. All of the primary works selected for examination were written to amuse the average, non-technical reader who knows little, if anything at all, about the field of linguistics, and who is probably oblivious to the very issues upon which the study centers. This supposition is important, because one of the present objectives is to point out the wealth of information about language that is readily available to everyone, but which too often goes unnoticed.

Interest in this study grew out of a Master's thesis on utopian fiction, which, I realized, appears now almost entirely in science fiction form. Science fiction-fantasy has a personality all its own, and the utopias and anti-utopias it contains have also assumed a character modern in style and presentation, even if traditional in ideology. Science fiction is "fictionalized science" only in the sense that its literary devices are often based on principles of the physical sciences—both theoretical and applied—and the stories it produces are quite often unofficial lessons in applied science. Linguistics, as a relative newcomer to the field of sciences, is probably the most poorly represented in the genre, at least in the technical sense. Writers of science fiction have done much over the past few decades to prepare modern man for the revolutionary changes inherent in our space age, and most average readers accept and understand scientific, technological terminology without question. But linguistics, even though it deals with a medium of communication vital to every human being, and one ages older than the most basic discovery of modern sciences, has done little to initiate modern readers into its processes and terminology. Language, when it appears in science fiction, is more likely to be in illustrative rather than instructional form, but even readers who have never been introduced to terms like "phoneme" and "immediate constituent" can nevertheless absorb information about the science of linguistics, if only they know what to look for.

But they must look for it in the literature of science fiction and fantasy. For reasons which will be clarified in the course of this examination, only fantasy literature which deals with the sciences in fictional form has the peculiar set of characteristics and capabilities that allow readers to acquire an effortless, yet quite technologically complex, education in modern sciences. One problem in attempting to demonstrate this theory, however, is that many readers who are accustomed to reading "good literature" may shy away from anything called "science fiction." It will not be my purpose here to defend this type of writing as "literature" or as a legitimate "genre" or to justify its existence. Other, better qualified writers have already done these things. The facts are, however, that science fiction is rapidly growing in popularity and literary potential, that authors in the field are very likely to have a vocation in one of the modern sciences, and, for those who can read it at all, it is habit-forming.

During the period of composition, I have corresponded with several of the authors whose writings will appear later, but of particular interest has been Charles F. Hockett, the only primary author whose selection is not science fiction. It is more aptly science fact, inasmuch as it involves no plot and no story, but is a technical and scholarly lesson in linguistics--and the main character is a Martian. My first letter to Dr. Hockett, in which I called science fiction "a genre still approached with caution by most scholars," prompted a generous reply from him, dated February 7, 1971, of which I quote a part:

> You say two things in your letter that disturb me a little. First, you say that science fiction is "a genre still approached with caution by most scholars"--true, indeed, of so-called literary scholars and related humanists, but not at all true of scholars in physical and biological science and in mathematics, who have participated in science fiction as readers and sometimes as writers for a long time. Norbert Wiener wrote some stories. Isaac Asimov, who has written a lot of science fiction, is a biochemist. It's only the litterateurs who shy away from it, and that is a reflection of the American version of Snow's "two cultures." The other point is that you imply that the linguistics in science fiction is sometimes sound. That is true--but only very rarely. Mainly a technical term or so is dropped to give the

iv

> illusion ("phoneme" started turning up about twenty-five years ago, for example). Mostly the linguistics is thoroughly unsound. The most unsoundest thing of all is the economical, efficiently-packaged "translator" or "language analysis machine" that is used to get human into contact with alien, or vice versa, quickly. As though everything in a language could be inferred logically from some small sample! Acquiring a language demands thousands of unrelated individual acts of learning; it just <u>isn't</u> a logical system that grows from elementary premises.

There are no translating machines within the scope of this study, but there are people who speak languages that do not actually exist. Rather, they speak what the author purports to be a language, and while he may not deal in the science of language study, he does provide a language which may be studied.

One of the major difficulties in dealing with science fiction is the unavailability--and often the complete absence--of research materials. Even when references to a specific item can be located, rare is the library that can supply a series of periodicals devoted to science fiction-fantasy. To compile a group of primary works such as those contained in this study, a researcher can depend only on his own reading in the field, hearsay, and serendipity. Notwithstanding, the problem here has not been the lack of primary selections, but an overabundance of them. Any reader who is interested in human speech and who is alert to the peculiarities and twists and alternate routes a language may assume, especially a reader who ventures into lands of imagination with imaginary speakers of make-believe languages, will begin to see the principles of language at work everywhere.

Many good primary selections have regretfully been omitted, but the short stories and novels included for examination have all been selected for a purpose; all of them contain an unusual illustration of some aspect of language, each being the best available example of its kind. All were chosen for their linguistic value and not their literary merit as a whole. Neither did the author's reputation enter into the selection of a single item, although it would occasionally seem so, inasmuch as many of the authors are educated men, scholars and teachers, authors of textbooks in various fields, and both writers and critics of serious literature. A surprising number of the authors hold Ph.D.'s and, purely by chance, some were discovered to be practicing linguists. Several appear in the dual role of science fiction writer and literary critic.

It should be emphasized that all sources are highly selective. Exhaustive bibliographies are available elsewhere, and only those meeting the needs of this study are included here. The entire content of this study, analyses of literary selections and methods and procedures, are directed toward the understanding of the average, non-technical reader rather than the trained linguist.

Readers of science fiction expect to find interplanetary rocket ships and time machines, adventures on distant planets and extra-terrestrial characters. Martians, Hobbits,

Venusians, rebellious computers, talking carrots--all will appear in the following pages, and it is important that the reader accept them in the spirit in which they were created. Of more importance is to examine what they say, how they say it, and why they say it that way. This is the province of linguistics.

CHAPTER I

INTRODUCTION

Linguistics, as compared to mathematics or biology, is a comparatively new addition to the field of sciences, and only within this century has it come to be called a "science." Linguistics is a descriptive science, as opposed to theoretical or applied sciences, but, like other fields, it has developed its own areas of specialization. It is assumed of fictional literature that only by special intent and for special purpose would an author violate the principles of mathematics by having two and two make five, or of biology in creating characters with three arms or seven fingers. This same supposition does not necessarily hold true for linguistic principles, however, inasmuch as linguistics as a science has not traditionally been a part of the school curriculum, and ordinary speakers of any language are generally unaware of the forces that have shaped their everyday speech.

One purpose of this study will be to examine imaginary languages created in modern fictional literature for their adherence to linguistic principles. Since all authors are not trained linguists, it would be of value to measure to what extent unconscious linguistic patterns are applied to the creation of fictional languages.

A second purpose will be to isolate areas of linguistic

specialization or application--historical linguistics, actual artificial language creation, anthropological linguistics, metalinguistics and semantics, and lexicography--and illustrate how each can be used as a literary device to enhance a particular theme, promote realism, or serve as a basis for an entire story.

A third purpose will be to propose more versatile uses of linguistics as a tool science in literary criticism.

In order to accomplish these purposes, it is necessary to include both fiction and nonfiction as source materials, although the nonfiction is not always of a referent or even a critical nature. For purposes of identification, "secondary sources" will indicate the nonfiction materials, and "primary sources" will refer only to the fictional selections. It is usually assumed that secondary sources are reference books, critical commentaries or reviews, and authoritative information referring specifically, by name, to certain primary sources; such is not the case in this study. For reasons that will become apparent later, authoritative information must be assembled not only through recognized texts written by known linguists, but also through the theories and speculations of non-linguists who have special insight into the workings of language. Only in rare instances will a secondary source mention a primary one by name; nonfictional secondary sources, in whatever medium they occur, are to be used here to establish a critical standard by which the languages in the primary, fictional selections can be evaluated.

Primary sources, the literary selections chosen for illustration and examination, are within the scope of modern literature. One dates from 1924, and two were written in the 1930's, but the majority were written after 1940. Predominating are those written within the last two decades. In form, both short stories and novels are used; without exception, these primary works all represent popular literature, as opposed to scholarly treaties, although several authors of primary sources also appear in their role of linguistic experts. Literary examples to be used here as illustrations have been selected on the basis of their linguistic value and not their literary merit, although the two are not mutually exclusive. The object of analysis is not the diction or literary skills of the author in relating his story, but the features of the imaginary language that he creates for his fictional, imaginary society to speak.

Every primary source contained here is science fiction, to some extent. Science fiction is a versatile literature, capable of producing poetry and its criticism (probably intergalactic in nature), history (hypothetical, of course), and any prose genre found in "mainstream" literature. Science fiction is not synonymous with "escape literature"; many literary classics are now claimed by science fiction. Several genres are represented in the selection of fictional illustrations presented here, but the genres themselves are important only because of the special literary features they hold in common that allow an author to create an imaginary language for use in a story. The language in James Joyce's Finnegan's Wake is noteworthy, and it is fictional, but it is not the type of imaginary language of concern here. Imaginative literature, or fantasy, is often set apart from pure fiction only by its connotative associations or by the indefinable "feel" of a story. There are several genres, however, whose basic literary features almost automatically turn simple fiction into fantasy, and all of the primary sources to be examined here have been produced by one of those genres.

One of the genres represented is utopian fiction, and selections of utopian fiction are identifiable by a set of standard literary devices that characterize the genre. While a social scientist might present his recommendations for better social organization in the form of a scholarly treatise, the same writer might sugarcoat his theories by illustrating them in operation among an imaginary society, and so produce a work of utopian fiction. Although utopian fiction is primarily intended as a social document, it is nevertheless embellished for popular reading, and there is a pattern of preliminary action that recurs predictably in this type of writing. Emphasis is on the social customs of the imaginary society, but the protagonist must be an outsider in order to provide a contrast of views. The device by which an author places his protagonist in the imaginary society--a plane crash in uncharted territory, interplanetary space travel, a shipwreck, a time machine, or variations of these--is incidental and may be disregarded as soon as the story begins. The protagonist arrives, meets inhabitants with whom he must establish a means of communication, and so either they are found to speak the same language or the protagonist quickly learns the native language. Then the story can begin.

A second genre, dystopian fiction, or sometimes called "anti-utopian," is an offspring of the utopian that has evolved during this century and has almost entirely replaced its predecessor in the field of fictional literature.[1] As a genre, dystopian fiction is a polemic literature. It is a social document in exactly the same sense as utopian fiction, but the message is simply carried in a different vehicle. While utopian fiction concerns an imaginary society that is "utopian" in the literal sense, dystopian fiction takes the same theories of the ideal, emphasizes and distorts them out of proportion, and creates a nightmarish world--what one critic calls "a utopia that backfired."[2] (Prominent in this genre are Brave New World, 1984, and Zamiatin's We, often called "the anti-utopian trilogy.") Social conditions are so

---

[1] Two books in exposition of this trend are Kingsley Amis's New Maps of Hell (New York: Harcourt, Brace and Company, 1960) and Chad Walsh's From Utopia to Nightmare (New York: Harper and Row, Publishers, 1962).

[2] Walsh, p. 13.

obviously distorted that an author, in this case, can depend upon the reader to provide the contrast in views and so has no need of the literary devices characteristic of utopian fiction. As a genre, however, it has its own literary pattern; the protagonist is not an outsider, but a member of the imaginary society who has been educated in, and environmentally conditioned by, its mores. The fictional citizens themselves think and speak in terms of what they believe, or have been taught to believe, is ideal. It is fatal for the protagonist, who is an average citizen, to possess above average reasoning power because, as he begins to rebel, he is destroyed by the system.

The differences between these two genres, utopian and dystopian, provide an interesting contrast in this study. Although both literary vehicles give an author the opportunity to create a language for his characters, the opportunities are not equal. Both types of societies usually explain their existence by including a review of history, with a holocaust of some type that virtually destroyed the world, leaving only a "saving remnant" to re-create civilization. The nature of the survivors dictates both the genre and the complexity of the social issues; good people create utopias and bad people create dystopias, and bad people and dystopian languages are always more interesting.

In addition to utopian and dystopian fiction, a third category of imaginative literature to be examined here is simple "escape" science fiction. Fictional selections in this category all have an element of fantasy, as well as imagination, and quite often an entire story takes place without the presence of a single <u>homo sapien</u>. The characters are people, but not necessarily human people. More often, however, both human beings and alien beings are concerned, and only selections of this type are used here. Science fiction, also called "space fiction" or "time and space fiction," is a genre with nebulous borders, and writers in the genre have become increasingly aware of its evolution during the past several decades. H. G. Wells is acknowledged as the "father of science fiction," and critics often quote passages from one of his books, such as this one from <u>War of the Worlds</u>, written in 1898:

> Those who have never seen a living Martian can scarcely imagine the strange horror of its appearance. . . . above all, the extraordinary intensity of the immense eyes . . . at once vital, intense, inhuman, crippled and monstrous. There was something fungoid in the oily brown skin, something in the clumsy deliberation of the tedious movements unspeakably nasty. Even at this first encounter, this first glimpse, I was overcome with disgust and dread.[3]

Passages such as this illustrate the type of writing that modern authors wish to dissociate themselves from, and modern science fiction is carefully delineated from the Wellsian with its sensationalism and "bug-eyed monsters" that dominated the genre until recently. Today, "the traditional Bug-Eyed

---

[3]Quoted in Amis, <u>New Maps of Hell</u>, p. 1.

Monster has become the symbol of the cheapest forms of science fiction, which meets its nadir in horror movies,"[4] and anyone who still thinks of science fiction in terms of sensationalism is apparently not aware of what has happened to the genre.

> Growing like a mushroom, science fiction has in a few years achieved the status of a major literary genre in its own right. It has hardly yet, however, been subjected to systematic investigation . . . . One expects science fiction to be particularly concerned with science. . . . It is surprising to find that this is not so. These systems of fantasy are, rather, preoccupied with communication . . . . The science fiction literature of the last few years offers an abundance of material to illustrate the various forms that the preoccupation with communication may take.[5]

To illustrate and investigate such theoretical forms of communication is one objective of this study. The purpose for having gone to some lengths to differentiate the characteristics of utopian, dystopian, and fantasy literature is to provide terminology and working materials for use throughout this study.[6] Either the term "science fiction" or "fantasy"

---

[4]Arthur C. Clarke, editor, Time Probe: The Sciences in Science Fiction (New York: Dell Publishing Company, 1967), p. 93. This statement is an editorial comment introducing one of the selections in this anthology.

[5]Robert Plank, "Communication in Science Fiction," The Use and Misuse of Language, S. I. Hayakawa, editor (Greenwich, Connecticut: Fawcett Publications, Inc., 1962), p. 143.

[6]The genres themselves blend and overlap, apparently causing frustration to editors of reference books as well as to researchers. One major reference, Reader's Guide to Periodical Literature, lists Brave New World under "Utopias," 1984 under simply "Fiction," and science fiction under "Science, fictional."

will be used to denote primary selections which are neither utopian nor dystopian in form or content, and to serve as a signal that these primary selections involve a very special type of imaginary, theoretical language. This is one instance in which analysis benefits by investigating the vocation, avocation, or special interests of the author.

It is to the advantage of most works of fiction for an author to set a story in an actual city, as an aid to realism, but when he wishes to present an idea for its speculative value alone, the element of fantasy allows him to create a "virginal territory" so that a reader can approach the idea without any preexisting standards associated with a specific time, locale, or race of people. Creating such "unreal estate"[7] often taxes the ingenuity of authors in keeping ahead of modern scientific knowledge. The New World was mysterious to Elizabethans, and H. G. Wells viewed Australia in the same way that the early twentieth century viewed Mars. Today, even Mars has lost its fascination to such an extent that authors must move beyond the bounds of Earth and into other galaxies and other periods of time in order to create a unique environment. The literary result is inevitably called science

---

[7]"Unreal estate" is the title later given to a taped interview, conducted by Kingsley Amis, with the late C. S. Lewis a few months before his death. The article appears in a chapter entitled "On Science Fiction" in C. S. Lewis's Of Other Worlds (New York: Harcourt, Brace and World, Inc., 1966), pp. 86-96, and as an introduction entitled "Unreal Estate" to Amis and Conquest's Spectrum 4: A Science Fiction Anthology (New York: Harcourt, Brace and World, Inc., 1965), pp. 13-22.

fiction, but these elaborate literary manipulations are given more attention than they deserve. They are traditional literary tools modernized. Still, they signal that the author has something of value to say quite apart from the actions comprising a plot, and that he wishes to stimulate thought rather than simply entertain. If he is a social scientist, a psychologist, or an anthropologist, either by vocation or avocation, the fictional society will probably be either utopian or dystopian. The personal interests of the author, especially if he is not a writer of fiction exclusively, determine the issues that are emphasized in the imaginary society.

Science fiction has been described as a literature for "people with technical training who want fictionalized shop talk."[8] While many writers ignore the issue of language altogether, a linguist-writer may choose to create an entire language system and build the society around it, just as a biologist-writer would give more attention to alien physiology. For this reason, the imaginary languages found in science fiction are more thoroughly explained and are superior because they are created by linguists who are fully aware of the linguistic principles involved, who choose this medium to explore theoretical possibilities. In doing so, they speak the language of science fiction, which has a vocabulary

---

[8] Amis, New Maps of Hell, p. 60.

of its own, including such words as <u>android</u>, <u>humanoid</u>, <u>space warp</u>, <u>hyperspace</u>, and the special term <u>terran</u> to denote an inhabitant of the planet Earth. Readers of science fiction understand such terms and expect them, and scholarly devotees of the genre recognize its unique need for neologisms.

"Exobiology" is not a recognized branch of biology. In the corpus of science fictional terminology, however, it is defined as "the study of life forms beyond the Earth, a science without a subject."[9] "Exolinguistics" would quite accurately describe the subject of this study--the study of the language of life forms beyond Earth. Both of these terms describe a science of speculation, using modern scientific knowledge, but just as the existence of other life forms cannot be proved, neither can it be disproved. Linguists might assume that all of the various languages now spoken on earth represent all the ways possible for a language system to be arranged, but that is only an assumption.

It could be claimed at this point that "other life forms" refers to imaginary beings in the allegorical or otherwise literary sense, but no such claim is offered. Elements of linguistic study have already proved valuable in the modern world, but the scope of this study will include the hypothesis that the examination of imaginary, non-existent

---

[9]Clarke, pp. 92-93. Linguistics is not one of the sciences included in this anthology.

languages--their phonetic and grammatical organization, their method of communication, and the possible relation between a culture and its language--may also have value. World events of the last few decades have taught twentieth-century man, if nothing else, not to laugh too loudly at Jules Verne. Fantasy is relative. As one leading linguist says, "What was prophecy--a willful, painful hope--thirty years ago is now as plainly attainable as a mere landing on the moon."[10] Jules Verne's fantasy, which was recorded in history books on July 20, 1969, is proof that theoretical scientists had long been working seriously on speculations.

Space travel is not fantasy, but it was when scientist-writers first began to speculate in the form of fantasy literature. Biologists have no "other life forms" to study, but they may apply their knowledge in the field to speculate on what chemical substances, other than carbon and nitrogen, could conceivably support life. The time might come when linguists will be called upon to analyze as yet unknown languages, perhaps involving a unique set of articulatory organs. In this event, they could profit by having paid attention to "make-believe" languages, particularly those created as speculation by their more imaginative scholarly colleagues, the exolinguists.

---

[10] I. A. Richards, So Much Nearer: Essays Toward a World English, 2nd ed. (New York: Harcourt, Brace and World, Inc., 1968), p. 5.

Linguistics is the science that studies language, but it is as yet a descriptive science. There is no area of specialization called "theoretical linguistics," but if there were, it would concern the imaginary languages contained in this study.

CHAPTER II

GROWTH OF LINGUISTIC REALISM IN FICTION

Realism in literature is a relatively new development, one which began as a literary movement only within the last century. It is the goal of modern writers of fiction to depict a scene as it would occur in real life and to make conversational exchanges as authentic as possible, with all of the errors and slang and improprieties that informal speech often includes. They are faced with the dual problem of creating an imaginary situation and then clothing it in the illusion of authenticity. Modern writers who set their stories in contemporary times have less of a problem than those who portray times past, in that such matters as surroundings and dress need not be mentioned. In fictional literature set in past eras, and particularly in stage productions, setting an authentic scene sometimes creates problems. Fashions of the period, furnishings, and even eating utensils must be appropriate to that period, as well as the speech habits of the characters, but this is only a technical difficulty requiring research. There is one problem involved in creative writing, however, which no amount of research can resolve into both realistic and satisfactory terms, but which rarely alarms even the most dedicated advocate of realism. That problem involves language.

Language is not particularly a problem if the characters are speaking English to an English-speaking audience, but if the characters are French and are supposedly speaking their own language, the problem of authenticity is insoluble. Either they speak in French, which will be unintelligible to a majority of the audience, or they speak in English, which is unrealistic. When two or more nationalities are present, it is acceptable that they will speak a common language (the language of the audience or reader) with accompanying accents to denote that they are foreign speakers, but it is entirely unrealistic that any one of them, when speaking with his fellow countrymen, will speak in the same "foreign" language simply for the benefit of the audience. This facet of creative writing rarely seems like a problem in realism because it has always been one area in which the "suspension of disbelief" operates automatically.

That this issue of linguistic realism is a universal one is evident in one of the first pieces of fiction known to the western world. Homer's characters are Greek and Trojan. At the time of the Trojan War, approximately 1200 B.C., the Greeks spoke a Mycenaean dialect of the evolving Greek language, and the Trojans presumably spoke Phrygian, a language quite different from Greek.[1]

---

[1] Because there is no record that the Trojans had a written language, scholars disagree as to the language that was spoken in Troy in 1200 B.C. They do agree that it was not Greek, however. See Leonard Cottrell, ed., "Minoan Scripts," Concise Encyclopedia of Archeology (New York: Hawthorne Books, Inc., 1960).

But in the Iliad, the two nationalities communicate with adequate understanding. The same situation occurs in the Aeneid, in which Phrygian-speaking Aeneas sails to the Punic-speaking land of Carthage and has no difficulty carrying on involved conversation with Queen Dido. In the eleventh-century Chanson de Roland, Arabic-speaking Moors and French-speaking Franks communicate with ease, although there is no mention of an interpreter. Such violations of authenticity apparently did not concern Homer or Virgil or the author of Chanson de Roland, but then neither is there any pretense that the situations or the events contained in their writings strive toward realism.

Dante, however, did use a less unrealistic approach at times, despite the allegorical framework of his Commedia. The suffering of the damned is real, and Dante is perhaps the first writer to illustrate an unknown language. At the depths of the Inferno, the fictional pilgrim Dante hears Plutus chant, "Papa Satán, Papa Satán, aleppe" (Canto VII, line 1), and Nimrod of the nethermost Titans bellows, "Rafel mahee amed zabi almit" (Canto XXXI, line 67), both utterances created for them in the Inferno. The "Papa Satán" phrase of Plutus's has a possible symbolic meaning in its original Italian, but as yet, no critic has found a single linguistic principle that helps to explain "aleppe."[2] The fictional guide Virgil

---

[2] "Papa" means Pope, rather than father; "Il papa santo" refers to the Pope, and so "papa Satán" is probably his opposite number. The Inferno, John Ciardi, trans. (New York: New American Library, 1954), p. 76.

acknowledges that Nimrod's utterance is gibberish which even the speaker cannot understand, but it is a most fitting speech for one symbolizing the Tower of Babel. Both of these examples of unknown languages within the fictional <u>Inferno</u> indicate an awareness of language on the part of the author. There are two levels of this awareness, however, because the pilgrim Dante and his guide, Virgil, are fictional characters. On the other level, the author Dante, in writing his <u>Commedia</u> in the fourteenth century, made no provisions for his Italian-speaking fictional self to communicate with his guide Virgil, who spoke the Latin of fourteen centuries previous to their journey. Yet there is no acknowledged linguistic problem in the poem.

By the end of the fourteenth century, there is some evidence that fiction writers were moving toward a less heroic portrayal of mankind in creating their characters, and perhaps Chaucer was one of the first to create realistic fictional characters by patterning many of his pilgrims after living persons. Not only did he give them human failings and foibles, but he reflected in them the bilingual society in which and for which he wrote. One of the most memorable descriptions of the prioress is the fact that she speaks the French of Stratford, but not the French of Paris. Further proof of Chaucer's attention to the linguistic habits of his characters is that in the fiction-within-fiction "Reeve's Tale," the two students speak in the dialect of Northern England. Although

Chaucer did not consistently transpose the sounds of their dialect, it is only for these two characters that he supplies conversation full of northern forms.³ Another use of regional dialect appears in the "Second Shepherd's Play," in which the rogue Mak affects a southern accent as a disguise. Used as a comic effect, his attempt does not deceive the first shepherd, who tells him to "unscrew his southern tooth" (Scene I). Either this play or Chaucer's "Reeve's Tale," both of whose dates are indefinite but which were written at approximately the same time, is probably the first known English fiction to use regional dialects in conversation.

A review of past scholarship up to this point in literary history would be very brief, considering only the criticism using linguistics as a tool science. There is little for scholars to work with, except for the phonetic transcriptions and Middle English dialect studies provided by Chaucer. One notable exception in medieval literature, The Travels of Sir John Mandeville, has provided the first lengthy, complicated, and controversial body of criticism, although it has not involved a great number of critics. This travel book, written probably during the last half of the fourteenth century or during the first few years of the fifteenth, is an autobiographical account of Mandeville's journey through several countries, most of which contain tribes of people without

---

³J. R. R. Tolkien, Transactions of the Philological Society, 1934, pp. 1ff.

heads, with only one large foot, or with other fantastic attributes. Of interest to linguistic scholars is that Mandeville includes an alphabet of the language supposedly spoken in the major countries. The presence of these alphabets, particularly two of them, has been valuable to textual linguists in attempting to identify the date, the author, and the original language of this book. Scribes began to simplify and abridge these alphabets with each succeeding copy, and the alphabets were omitted altogether by the time the first printed version was made. Therefore, recension studies were based almost entirely on the number and intricacy of the hieroglyphs in the alphabets instead of on any aspect of word transcription. The alphabets have also provided material for comparative linguists, who have attempted to verify Mandeville's information. Mandeville identifies each alphabet with a language and a country, and scholars have discovered that his "Greek" is an amalgamation of six ancient alphabets, his "Egyptian" is based on Coptic, his "Saracen" is actually a corrupted runic alphabet; all but two of his supposed authentic alphabets were based on actual languages. These two, Cathay and Pentexoire, are still mysteries. For Pentexoire, the language spoken in the land of the famous Prester John, Mandeville also includes a table of equivalent English letters and a phonetic pronunciation for each hieroglyph. Mandeville used a great measure of imagination in supplying all of the alphabets, but assuming that the

Pentexoire is totally a fabrication, this seems to be the first literary attempt to create the rudiments of an entirely imaginary language.[4]

From that time, there seems to have been a growing awareness on the part of authors that the linguistic habits of their characters could be an additional tool in literary skill. For the most part, authors reflected their own knowledge or interests into the fictional language of their characters. Sir Thomas More, in his Preface to Utopia, describes himself as "a man better sene in the Greke language, then in the Latin tongue"; his narrator in the book, Raphaell Hythlodaye, is "very well lerned in the Latine tongue; but profounde and excellent in the Greke language."[5] The Utopian people, according to Hythloday, saw little value in Latin writers, but asked to be taught Greek so that they could read Greek literature. Their language, Hythloday reports, indicates that the Utopian nation might have had its beginning with the Greeks "bycause their speche, which in al other poyntes is not much unlyke the Persian tonge, kepeth dyvers signes and tokens of the Greke

---

[4]Malcolm Letts, Sir John Mandeville: The Man and his Book (London: The Batchworth Press, 1949). Chapter XVII, "The Alphabets," is the product of the author and G. D. Painter, and it includes a full discussion of the alphabets, pertinent manuscripts, and a summary of scholarship.

[5]Sir Thomas More, Utopia, J. Rawson Lumby, ed. (Cambridge: Cambridge University Press, 1879), p. 19. This is a reprint of Hearne's edition of 1716, which was based on the first edition translation by Raphe Robynson in 1556.

langage in the names of their cityes and of theire magistrates."[6] Because of the varied prefatory material and the several afterwords to Utopia, there are several points of view represented, but the book manages to include references to the Utopian language from at least four sources: from More himself as the author, from Hythloday as the narrator and first-person observer, from Peter Giles, who addresses this entire epistle to Jerome Buslid, and from the printer of the first English edition. In the original Latin edition, More included an alphabet of the Utopian language, the characters formed of circles and squares, with lines drawn either wholly or partly through them, a triangle also representing one letter and certain angles and curves the rest.[7] He then wrote a four-line verse in these characters and gave a Latin translation of the Utopian lines. The first English translator, Raphe Robynson, translated the Latin into English, but omitted the Utopian characters; in one of the afterwords, however, Peter Giles attempted this version of transcribing the four lines, using English letters:

Utopos ha Boccas Peula Chama Polta Chamaan.
Bargol he maglomi Baccan foma gymnosophaon.
Agrama gymnosophon labarem bacha bodamilomin.

---

[6] Ibid., p. 118.

[7] Ibid., editor's note on p. 231. The alphabet itself is not reprinted in this edition; description of the characters is the editor's.

Voluala barchin heman la lauoluala dramme pagloni.[8]

This transcription is entirely the product of Peter Giles, inasmuch as More gave no equivalent English letters to his Utopian characters. The fourth reference was appended to the first English edition by its printer, Abraham Veale, who made this apology:

> The Utopian alaphabete, good reader, whiche in the above written epistle is promised, hereunto I have not now adjoyned, because I have not as yet the true characters or fourmes of the Utopiane letters. And no marveill, seying it is a tongue to us muche straunger then the Indian, the persian, the Syrian, the Arabicke, the Egyptian, the Macedonian, the Sclavonian, the Ciprian, the Scythian etc. Which tongues though they be nothing so straunge among us, as the Utopian is, yet their characters we have not. But I trust, God willing, at the next impression hereof, to perfourme that whiche nowe I cannot, that is to saye, to exhibite perfectly unto thee, the Utopian alphabete. . . .[9]

Peter Giles' transcription of the verse cannot be attributed to More, but it is significant that More, in his attempt to give realistic evidence of the Utopian language, created such enthusiasm and interest. Its omission from the printed version was due to a technical difficulty in type setting, but the printer evidently considered it important enough to warrant apology. Even though More provided an alphabet for

---

[8] Ibid., p. 170. Peter Giles admitted to his fabrication in a letter to Buslidius, p. 227a of the *Vita et Obitus Thomae Mori* (Frankfort, 1689). The editor calls it "a verse in a barbarous language," p. 237.

[9] Ibid., p. 172.

the Utopians, he did not choose to illustrate the Utopian
language in their conversation, and so there is no record
of the nature of that fictional language in operation. Had
he illustrated the Utopians using words of the language, instead of simply describing it, scholars could have tested the
validity of the claim that its basis was Greek.

Apart from purposely invented fictional languages for
fictional characters to speak, authors could reflect their
own observations about contemporary speech into the speech
of their characters. The principal result was the use of
various regional dialects, inasmuch as the center of culture
in sixteenth-century England was London, London was subject
to many linguistic influences from outside the area, and most
writers were daily exposed to examples of these dialectical
differences. Ben Jonson, in his The Tale of a Tub, introduces a Southern countryman who speaks in a rural English
Southern accent featuring mostly the voicing of s and f to z
and v. There is some indication that Shakespeare included
some idiosyncrasies of the Warwickshire accent into his writings,[10] but he utilized even more successfully the bilingual
society that was contemporary to some of his historical plays.

Historical records indicate that both French and English
were spoken fluently during the days of Henry V, and

---

[10]Margaret Schlauch, The English Language in Modern Times
(since 1400) (Warszawa: Panstwowe Wydawnictwo Naukowe, 1959),
p. 85. Dr. Schlauch is a professor of English philology at
the University of Warsaw, where this book was published.

Shakespeare makes use of this fact in having his characters alternate between the two languages. The possibilities are thus increased for polyglot puns, as in the case of the comic characters Gower and Fluellen, who can supply Welsh and Scottish accents as well. The features of Fluellen's accent are established throughout the play, as he says "crossing the pridge" (Act III, scene 6), "fortune is plind" (Act III, scene 6), his "pest friend" and "intoxicates his prains" (Act IV, scene 7). So the scene is set for the pun:

> Flu. Ay, he was porn at Monmouth, Captain Gower. What do you call the town's name, where Alexander the Pig was born?
>
> Gow. Alexander the Great.
>
> Flu. Why, I pray you, is not pig, great? The pig, or the great, or the mighty, or the huge, or the magnanimous, are all one reckonings, save the phrase is a little variations.
> (Act IV, scene 7)

Except for a few inconsistencies in Fluellen's speech, such as his "at such a breach . . . who came off bravely" (Act III, scene 6), Shakespeare prepared for the polyglot pun utilizing the difference between a voiced and an unvoiced bilabial. Much comment has been caused, also, by the delightful little scene between Katharine of France and her maid, which is conducted almost entirely in French. Shakespeare has effectively used phonetic spelling which conveys both ladies' mispronunciation of English words according to the corresponding sounds or lack of them in French. Another pun is possible because of the word <u>foot</u>, which has a similar pronunciation in both languages, but not the same definition.

After the Renaissance, scholars began to develop interest in the internal operation of language. Jonathan Swift employed something akin to a "literary idiolect" in his "little language" of <u>Letters of Stella</u>.[11] Further examples of his interest in language appear throughout <u>Gulliver's Travels</u>, in which he utilizes the elements of several invented languages. Apparently Swift had insight into which areas of this fictional adventure would most appeal to the readers' sense of logic and which would be accepted as fantasy. It is mentioned that Gulliver, upon his arrival in Laputa, "learned the language" of the Lilliputians; each fictional country in the book has its own language, in fact, and it is to be assumed that all of the reported conversations take place in one of the languages Gulliver is forced to learn during his travels. Swift did not explain the process by which Gulliver deciphered that completely foreign language without benefit of an interpreter, but at least he did not expect the reader to believe that a race of intelligent horses would speak perfect eighteenth-century English.

It was not until 1923 that modern linguistic scholarship looked seriously at Swift's "horse language." In his critical

---

[11]This idiolect is of biographical nature and, therefore, not pertinent to this study. For reference, see Elrington Ball, <u>The Correspondence of Jonathan Swift</u>, 6 vols. (London: Bell Publishers, Ltd., 1910-1914), III, 777; V, 188-193.

biography of Swift, William A. Eddy applied certain principles of metathesis and syllable reversals, those principles used more obviously in the personal letters to Stella, and arrived at a basis for many of the place names in Gulliver's Travels. He examined the phonetic construction of the Houyhnhyn language and discovered that it differed in definite points from the other three languages represented in the book. It is composed mostly of labials, nasals, and glides, sounds that are easy to make with little dexterity of the tongue, distinctive for their onomatopoeic value and consistent with the whinny-producing vocal chords of a horse.[12] Other scholars examined the words representing the Trildrogdribian, Brobdingnagian, and Lilliputian languages, and they discovered that Swift had ingeniously used a method of metathesis, dissimilation and assimilation, word- and syllable-reversal, anagrams, and addition of key letters to form the examples of his fictional languages; but they also discovered that Swift had used several modern languages--Greek, Hebrew, French, German, Italian, and Spanish--as a basis for his fabricated languages.[13] In addition, the languages have been examined separately to determine the pattern of each and the method used by Swift. The Laputian language uses mostly voiced, rather than unvoiced,

---

[12]Wm. A. Eddy, Gulliver's Travels: A Critical Study (New York: Russell and Russell, Publishers, 1963), p. 218. This is a reprint of the 1923 edition.

[13]Ronald Smith, "Swift's Little Language and Nonsense Names," JEGP, LIII (April, 1954), 178-96.

consonants; it is a smooth language because most of the vowels are long. The Trildrogdribian language is composed of closed syllables containing short vowels, causing it to sound choppy and staccato. The Houyhnhyn tongue, as has been mentioned, contains only one example of a hard g, but otherwise, is suitable to the vocal apparatus of a horse.[14] Thus the phonetic and morphological constituents of these fictional languages have been seriously examined under the principles of modern linguistic study, and they have been found to be valid. However, it might be interesting to read the report of a linguistic anthropologist, comparing the composition of a language to the people who speak that language in the book; the choppy and staccato language of the Trildrogdribians, for example, might indicate that the people are hyperactive, quick and impulsive in their actions, and perhaps disconnected in their thoughts. If this were the case, it would prove attention to realism in yet another field of criticism.

It is obvious, of course, that complete linguistic realism is impossible, especially in those works in which, ideally, the reader should be reading conversation in a language created by and known only to the author himself. Concessions

---

[14]H. D. Kelling, "Some Significant Names in Gulliver's Travels," Studies in Philology, XLVIII (1951), 761-78. This long and valuable article summarizes past scholarship on the languages in Gulliver's Travels through 1950, giving a bibliography and annotating each item. Kelling takes issue with some of Eddy's previous conclusions and discredit's Eddy's claim to the first critic to give attention to Swift's invented languages.

must be made in the interest of the reader, but the author may choose one of three means by which it is possible to convey the idea that his characters are speaking in some tongue other than that of the reader.

First, the author may actually use the English language as a basis, but alter the morphological or syntactical elements to produce a basic language unlike modern English, but comprehensible to English-speaking readers.

Second, when the fictional language is non-English and the author wishes to stress its phonetic system or its ability to compound morphemes into a variety of combinations, or perhaps when he simply wishes to keep the reader aware that the characters are speaking in another language, certain key words will always be used in that tongue. He might say, for example, "The old <u>kala</u> wearily entered his <u>shambla</u>, slipped his dusty <u>mekuls</u> from his feet, and took a drink of <u>pol</u>." Such key words will always appear in the foreign tongue, and soon the reader will begin to register them automatically without thinking of them as translated words. A skillful author will include a variety of these key words, always defining them through their context instead of offering an actual definition, so that he may eventually combine them into other compounds and actually "teach" the reader his fictional language.

Or, third, if the major importance of the language is its content alone, the author may choose to ignore the fictional sounds and word formation altogether and relate the entire content in English. The only logical explanation given is that, as often happens in science fiction, the characters are communicating with thought waves or light signals or other equally irrelevant means. This method has more linguistic possibilities than are apparent at first, however, especially in the field of semantics. If the author assumes that a "thought wave," whatever that may be, can communicate only clear-cut ideas without provision for idioms, connotations, inflectional variations, or words of aesthetic appreciation, then the resulting conversations should more than illustrate the importance of semantics as an element of language.

Chapter III

LINGUISTIC NOVELTIES AND MODERN FICTION

Gathering momentum since the 1930's, the element of grammar in linguistics has become a descriptive system, in conjunction with the usage movement, as opposed to the old "prescribe and proscribe" method with its list of rules guaranteed to produce "error free" writing and speaking. Usage, which considers language as it is used by native speakers, does not carry the labels "correct" or "incorrect" into such an ambivalent area as human speech. Instead, it simply considers the appropriateness or acceptability of a given expression or grammatical form, in the context of occasion, cultural levels and interest, subject matter, and other environmental factors of both speaker and listener.[1] With these new criteria, certain words or phrases may be labeled "standard" or "substandard," and generally it is only a person thoroughly schooled in the older, traditional grammar who will sacrifice clarity or fluency in order to avoid splitting an infinitive or ending a sentence with a preposition.

---

[1] Two excellent short summaries will be found in H. A. Gleason's Linguistics and English Grammar (New York: Holt, Rinehart and Winston, Inc., 1965), pp. 15-19, and in Mario Pei's "A Loss for Words," Saturday Review, XLVII (November 14, 1964), 82-84.

Today's new "rules" of language are those allowing the most accurate and expressive communication between speaker and spoken-to, and this new set of criteria has demanded a new look at grammar.

It is not inappropriate to mention descriptive grammar as a "linguistic novelty" because, no doubt, many parents have looked in bewilderment at their children's "new-fangled" grammar books and heard them speak of "kernel sentences" and "structure signals" and "phrase-structure rules" and other strange things. To one expecting the old exercises in subject-verb agreement, this is indeed a new type of grammar.

With this "new grammar" has come new terminology, as modern grammarians have abandoned the traditional eight parts of speech. Instead of insisting that every word in the English language fall neatly into one of the eight categories, modern grammarians begin the classification of words from the opposite end. They have set up groups called "form classes," into which words will automatically fall according to their form, function, or position in a sentence. Such a process of classification is likely to make use of the "slot-filler" or "slot-and-filler" technique:

   The _____ played a _____

Any word which can fill either of the vacant slots is a Form Class I word (a traditional grammarian would probably call it a noun), and other form class words can be identified in a similar manner.

Structural grammarians often invent nonsense sentences to illustrate the significance of "structure signals" in a sentence, or they quote Lewis Carroll's "Jabberwocky"--a poem Hockett describes as "a grammatical skeleton which Lewis Carroll clothed with flesh in the form of nonsense-syllables":[2]

      'Twas brillig, and the slithy toves
      Did gyre and gimble in the wabe;
      All mimsy were the borogoves,
      And the mome raths outgrabe.

Disregarding the nonsense words, here are the structure signals in this poem:

      'Twas __(1)__, and the __(2)__y __(3)__s
      Did __(4)__ and __(5)__ in the __(6)__;
      All __(7)__y were the __(8)__s,
      And the __(9)__ __(10)__s __(11)__.

Structure signals are the "bones" of the grammatical skeleton, and while the slots may be filled in to provide the lexical features of the sentence, each slot will accommodate only a certain type of "form class" word. Using traditional terminology, slots (1) and (2) will be filled by adjectives, slot (3) by a plural noun, slots (4) and (5) by verbs and so on. (Humpty Dumpty identifies *outgrabe* as the past tense of the verb *outgribe*, and so the last slot will be filled by a past tense verb.) While any appropriate word can be used to fill the slots, Hockett supplies these two examples:

---

    [2]Charles F. Hockett, *A Course in Modern Linguistics* (New York: The Macmillan Company, 1958), pp. 262-264. (Carroll's *Alice's Adventures in Wonderland*, in which "Jabberwocky" appears, was written in 1865.)

>'Twas morning, and the merry sunbeams did glitter and
>dance in the snow; all tinselly were the treetops,
>and the happy fairies frolicked.
>
>'Twas stormy, and the tall pines did quiver and tremble
>in the gale; all dark were the streets, and the weary
>villagers slept.³

"Jabberwocky" is readable, if not comprehensible, because of its structure signals, but Lewis Carroll obviously did not write the poem for the benefit of philologists, who would not quote it for this purpose until almost a century later. Carroll wrote it for fun. The fact that philologists, or linguists, of a later century find it structurally and grammatically sound attests only to Carroll's literary and linguistic skills. In his day, such analysis would have been the province of a philologist, but today, that of a linguist.

It is only a matter of terminology. The term "philologist" is fast becoming obsolete in favor of "linguist," inasmuch as modern linguistic study ranges far beyond the study of words, as the derivation of "philology" indicates. In former decades when "philology" and "philologist" were the accepted terms in this science, "linguist" was used to denote one who could speak several languages, but historical evolution of usage has reassigned the term "linguist" in a more accurately definitive sense--a specialist in the study of language. To fill its former slot, "polyglot" now refers to a speaker of many lan-

---

³Ibid.

guages.[4] The total evolution of these terms is far from complete, however, and readers should be prepared to accept philologist-linguist and linguist-polyglot as possible synonyms, depending on context.

A linguist is a specialist in the study of language, but becoming a linguist does not necessarily demand the prerequisite of university training in the same sense as becoming a surgeon or a nuclear physicist. Language is all around us, available for study, and anyone with curiosity and interest and imagination can observe the realm of language in action. A knowledge of scholarship on the subject is available, now more than ever before, because evidence of linguistic scholarship appears outside of scholarly journals and scholarly conferences. Modern writers, especially, recognize the potential of language as a "playground" and a versatile literary device, using language for its comic effects as well as its serious ones.

There are, of course, Ogden Nash and Bill Nye and Artemus Ward. And a convenient prose vehicle for authors who want to "play" with language is a familiar nursery rhyme or fairy tale. The reader already knows the plot, so he can concentrate on

---

[4]Cynthia D. Buchanan, *A Programed Introduction to Linguistics* (Boston: D. C. Heath and Company, 1963), p. 1. See also Benjamin Lee Whorf, "Science and Linguistics," *Language and Culture: A Reader*, Patrick Gleeson and Nancy Wakefield, eds. (Columbus, Ohio: Charles E. Merrill Publishing Company, 1968), pp. 43-44.

the words. The "near-phonetics" H. L. Chace uses to tell the old favorites in <u>Anguish Languish</u> is an example:

Ladle Rat Rotten Hut

> Wants pawn term dare worsted ladle gull hoe lift wetter murder inner ladle cordage honor itch offer lodge, dock florist. Disk ladle gull orphan worry putty ladle rat cluck wetter ladle rat hut, an fur disk raisin pimple colder Ladle Rat Rotten Hut.
> Wan moaning Ladle Rat Rotten Hut's murder colder inset.
> "Ladle Rat Rotten Hut, heresy ladle basking winsome burden barter an shirker cockles. Tick disk ladle basking tutor cordage offer groin-murder hoe lifts honor udder site offer florist. . . . Dun daily-doily inner florist, an yonder nor sorghum-stenches, dun stopper torque wet strainers!"[5]

The only "strainer" that she meets is the "wicket woof"; he rushes to the "groin-murder's cordage," where he "garbled erupt" before Ladle Rat Rotten Hut arrives. "On-forger-nutly," she fails to recognize him in her grandmother's "nut cup an gnat-gun," and he also "garbled erupt." The "mural" of the story is that "Yonder nor sorghum-stenches shut ladle gulls stopper torque wet strainers."

Dave Morrah tells "Mein Grossfader's Rhymers und Fables" in Twisted Teutonic, or Deutch Double-talk:

---

[5] H. L. Chace, <u>Anguish Languish</u> (Englewood Cliffs, New Jersey: Prentice-Hall, Inc., 1956), pp. 19-22. The book also contains selections for poetry and music lovers--"Casing Adder Bet," "Fur Hazy Jelly Gut Furlough," "Hormone Derange," and others.

Beauty und das Beast

  Ein grosser beast mit tushentoothers und flamisch eyeballen ben kidnappen ein beautischer fraulein. Ach! Der fraulein ben homensickisch mit screamen und wailen. Finalisch, das beast ben upfedden mit der yellen und releasen der beauty.

  Soonisch after der fraulein ist departen, das beast ben obercomen mit yearnen und wanten der beauty ist returnen. Also der fraulein is deciden, "Beneathen der uglischer outercoaten ein softisch heart ben gethumpen."

  Himmel! Der beauty ben returnen und finden das beast is downcasten mit gloomerpussen. Mit quickisch rushen der fraulein ben grabben das beast und onputten der lippenkissen!

  Ach, du lieber! Mit der kissen ein magickerspelle ben broken, und der beauty ist becomen ein beast mit tushentoothers und flamisch eyeballen![6]

Morrah also includes "Heinrich Schnibble's Deutcher Wordenbooke," with some of the following definitions:

  Golf course---Hittenhuntenfield
  Golf clubs---Hittenhuntenfielderhittensticks
  Golfer---Hittenhuntenfielderhittenstickenswinger
  Clubhouse---Hittenhuntenfielderhittenstickenswingerstart-
     enstoppenplatz[7]

  Kingsley Amis takes as one of the theses in his <u>New Maps of Hell</u> the idea that there is too little humor in science fiction. As a popular writer himself, he often adds comic

---

  [6]Dave Morrah, <u>Der Wizard in Ozzenland</u> (New York: Modern Literary Editions Publishing Company, 1962), p. 10. Morrah's "Grossfader" fables began appearing as a regular feature in <u>The Saturday Evening Post</u> in the 1940's.

  [7]<u>Ibid.</u>, p. 73.

touches to his stories, and quite often, the comic element comes in the form of an imaginary language. "Hemingway in Space"[8] is the story of an outer space "xeeb" hunt to test the virility of the hero, an elderly Martian guide whom the hero addresses "in the archaic Martian courtly tongue," and a heroine and a literary style that are clever caricatures of Hemingway.

Such examples of "fun with language" are found often in popular fiction, if the reader is alert to linguistics as a literary device. An even more complex and effective use of linguistic principles can be found in fantasy fiction when the reader, particularly one who is accustomed to more scholarly reading, can learn to appreciate the genre for its unique advantages. Scholarly devotees of science fiction, in a paranoic attempt to justify the genre, trace its beginnings back to Lucian of Samosata, whose second-century True History includes the first known account of an interplanetary voyage.[9] But the truth is that creating a simple sense of wonder has been the task of writers of fiction throughout history. Setting a story in a virgin territory is actually a consideration of real geography. Whatever portion of the world is known to man is automatically excluded; this indicates that in the twentieth

---

[8]Kingsley Amis, "Hemingway in Space," 6th Annual Edition of the Year's Best Science Fiction and Fantasy, Judith Merril, ed. (New York: Dell Publishing Co., Inc., 1962), pp. 323-328.

[9]Amis, New Maps of Hell, p. 27.

century, the planet Earth is no longer interesting, and recently, the moon began its decline as a potential locale for a fantasy story. Thus, modern writers relocate in other worlds, and possibly in other galaxies, abandoning "space" for "hyperspace" in order to justify the existence of an entirely unique environment.

J. R. R. Tolkien believes that no such justification is necessary; it is sufficient to acknowledge that the tale is a fantasy, a myth, a fairy story. The reader's imagination will take over, or he will close the book.[10] Tolkien places strict limitations upon the creative-fantasy story, however. The "fantastic" elements in the story, whether illustrative or merely decorative, must be of a simple and fundamental nature--stones, trees, flowers, everyday acts, familiar objects--but as seen through the eyes of wonder.[11] A practitioner of his own theories, Tolkien has created probably the most prodigious adult fantasy story in the history of literature and one which more than amply illustrates the present state of linguistic realism in modern literature.

Tolkien's fantasy trilogy, The Lord of the Rings, creates races of Elves, Dwarves, "halflings" called Hobbits, Trolls, Ents, Orcs, plus other creatures, and in the course of the

---

[10] J. R. R. Tolkien, "On Fairy Stories," The Tolkien Reader (New York: Ballentine Books, Inc., 1966), pp. 3-84.

[11] Ibid., p. 59.

six-book adventure (each volume contains two books), Tolkien not only invents a language for each of the races; he illustrates the use of each language by its race of speakers, often writing entire poems in the imaginary languages and then rendering them into English. Volume III, entitled <u>The Return of the King</u>, contains six subdivided appendixes that give an almost unbelievably detailed account of his mythical land and its inhabitants--maps, geneological tables, history, folklore, and, of course, language. Of particular interest to this study are Appendix E, "Writing and Spelling," and Appendix F, "The Languages and People of the Third Age." The language of the Hobbits, called Westron, or Common Speech, is the accepted standard language throughout the land, but in evidence are at least six other languages, including both Low Elven (called simply Elvish) and High Elven, also called Quenya. Appendix E contains tables of alphabetic script for three of the languages, complete with a history of their development, and detailed phonetic descriptions and examples of both vowels and consonants in each language. Appendix F contains a linguistic history of each language, factors in linguistic relativity among his peoples, peculiarities existing in any single language, and the derivation of place names and personal names.

There is no hint of "tongue in cheek" in Tolkien's linguistic analysis of his imaginary languages, and the reader often forgets that such languages and their speakers do not exist. Anyone who knows Tolkien as a scholar of Old English can easily compare his scholarly thoroughness in this analysis with that of his critical works on Beowulf.

Evidence of Tolkien's interest in Old English appears in one of the tribes, the Riders of Rodan, or the Rohirrim. He states, in Appendix F, "The language of Rohan I have accordingly made to resemble ancient English, since it was related both (more distantly) to the Common Speech, and (very closely) to the former tongue of the northern Hobbits. . . ."[12] Critic John Tinker has identified some of the Old English elements in personal names, place names, names of objects and animals, and the use of words and phrases in the language of the Rohirrim.[13] An Old English word for "horse" is eoh, and one of the first references to the people is Éotheod, Old English þeod meaning "tribe, nation, people." The Riders of Rodan are indeed a "horse people," and many of their personal names reflect their horsemanship--Éomer, Éomund, Éowyn, Éothain--with other names deriving from OE mere ("mare") and mearh ("horse, steed"). Other names are Théoden (OE þeoden means "prince, king"), Thengel (from OE þengel, "prince"), and their mother Théodwyn, "joy of princes"; one of Gandalf the Grey's names is Grayhame, from OE graeghama, literally

---

[12]J. R. R. Tolkien, The Return of the King (New York: Ballentine Books, Inc., 1965), p. 517.

[13]John Tinker, "Old English in Rohan," Tolkien and the Critics (Notre Dame, Indiana: University of Notre Dame Press, 1969), p. 164-169.

meaning "gray covering."[14] Tinker points specifically to two phrases spoken in the language of the Rohirrim: Éomer's speech includes the phrase, "Westu Théoden hál!" (Volume II, p. 122), and his daughter Éowyn, in offering wine to the king, says, "Ferthu Théoden hál!" These phrases translate, "Be thou healthy, Théoden!" and "Go thou Théoden healthy!" The language of Rohan not only "resembles" Old English, it is Old English.[15]

Among the many areas in The Lord of the Ring trilogy that lend themselves well to literary criticism are the names of the characters, which are as euphonious as poetry, and the poetry itself that abounds in all three volumes. Critic Neil Isaacs comments that although the inclusion of much poetry is one of the important aspects of the narrative, no one as yet has attempted to evaluate the poems for their own value or for the way they operate in context.[16] Of special interest in the scope of this study are several poems written in the Elvish language and translated into English, all appearing in Volume I, The Fellowship of the Ring. Most poems are not given titles, as characters break into lyric poetry as a natural means of

---

[14]Ibid., p. 165.

[15]Ibid., p. 169.

[16]Neil D. Isaacs, "On the Possibility of Writing Tolkien Criticism," Tolkien and the Critics, p. 8.

expression. One exception is "A Elbereth Gilthoniel" (Volume I, Book 2, Chapter 1), written in the High Elven speech called Quenya.

> A Elbereth Gilthoniel,
> silivren penna míriel
> o menel aglar elenath!
> Na-chaered palan-díriel
> o galadhremmin ennorath,
> Fanuilos, le linnathon
> nef aear, sí nef aearon![17]

Although this study will not attempt such an analysis, it would be interesting to take examples in the Elvish language, such as the poems (Volume I, pages 205, 250, and 394) and the long phrases with English translations (Volume I, pages 90, 319, and 320, plus others in Volumes II and III), and using the English translations for comparative purposes, attempt to establish a descriptive outline of Elvish lexicon morphology, and syntax.

The Lord of the Rings is listed here as a linguistic novelty for several reasons. First, its length alone almost precludes classifying it with novels and short stories that make up the body of primary sources for examination. The average novel rarely exceeds 300 pages, and Tolkien's trilogy has approximately 1500 pages. A second reason is that the trilogy is not typical of modern popular literature. It is far superior in exemplifying the techniques of linguistic

---

[17] J. R. R. Tolkien, The Fellowship of the Ring (Boston: Houghton-Mifflin Co., 1967), p. 250.

creation, and it is somewhat unfair to compare the competency of the average modern writer to the linguistic mastery of Tolkien with his many decades of scholarly study. In short, The Lord of the Rings is atypical because it is too good for the purpose of this study.

A third reason for considering the trilogy a novelty is that many of the songs and poems contained in it have been recorded and released as a popular record. Songs have been set to music and sung by William Elvin, and Tolkien himself recites "A Elbereth Gilthoniel" and other poems in Elvish. Even with the excellent phonetic description that is included at the end of the trilogy, only the creator of an imaginary language knows exactly how it should be spoken. Tolkien, now nearing eighty, speaks it with authority and, it seems, with affection. The back of the record jacket includes an introduction by W. H. Auden, who says,

> Nobody could have written . . . The Lord of the Rings who was not both a philologist and a poet. For example, only a philologist, and an exceptional one at that, could have invented an 'imaginary' language for the Elves which has all the properties of a 'real' one. . . . On this record you will have the pleasure of hearing him recite a poem in Elvish. I wish there had been grooves enough to permit the inclusion of something by a Rohan poet.[18]

---

[18] J. R. R. Tolkien, Poems and Songs of Middle Earth, music composed and sung by William Elvin, piano accompanyment by David Swann (New York: Caedmon TC 1231, 1967). Available in stereo and monaural.

CHAPTER IV

HISTORICAL LINGUISTICS AND HYPOTHETICAL HISTORY

Fictional history is an integral part of fantasy literature, particularly in utopian fiction, because the imaginary society is a direct result of certain historical events. Virtually every utopian (and its counterpart, dystopian) work contains a summary of its past fictional history. Not all such works deal with an alteration of language, and those that do show differences in the imaginary language do not always contain a linguistic history to explain its development. But a language, like a nation, has its heritage. While the two histories--national and linguistic--might be parallel in some aspects, they are interdependent only to a point. For example, America, as a territory, dates its national history from colonial times or perhaps from 1492, but the language spoken in America has a linguistic history extending many centuries before its existence as a nation. American English, as it is spoken in 1971, is not like the English spoken by King Alfred in 900, but it is the same language as it has changed in its constant usage through time.

That a living language changes through the years is a recognized fact. Analyzing the causes for such changes and the specific changes themselves is within the province of historical linguistics, an interdisciplinary science in which each discipline contributes its share. History, in a selective process, identifies events in the "external," or outer history of a language that were significant in causing alterations in speech. Linguistics, applied to the "internal," or inner history, allows for the systematic tracing of those alterations through time to discover the linguistic heritage of a language. The outer history must necessarily be a selective process in that all historical events do not affect a language, regardless of their value to a historian. Columbus's discovery in 1492, for example, is of less interest to a historical linguist than is Caxton's printing press less than two decades earlier because of the impact of printing as a stabilizing force on the English language. The Norman invasion of England is only another chronological event to a pure historian, but it is of paramount interest to a linguist because the French culture and French language of the conquering Normans overshadowed those of the conquered English for several centuries, after which time English emerged much changed.

In the dichotomy of historical linguistics--the outer and the inner history--the latter is by far the more complex. The impact of one single historical event can produce permanent effects in introducing new vocabulary or new sounds, in changing the pronunciation of existing words, in causing the systematic mutation of entire classes of sounds, or in revolutionizing the system of orthography. These changes occur so slowly, however, and in such indefinite states, that the events of outer history with their specific dates provide a more accurate measure by which the periods of both English literature and English language are identified.

The periods of English language are Old English, Middle English, and Modern English; the dates 500, 1100, and 1500 are simply a convenient rounding off of the years 449, 1066, and 1475--the dates of the Germanic invasion of England, the Norman conquest of England, and the introduction of printing into England. The selection of each of these specific events of history as the beginning of a new period in linguistic development has been arbitrary, but generally unchallenged. It is logical at this point to wonder what event future historical linguists will choose to represent the end of the Modern English period and what title they will give to the succeeding period when the term "modern" will be an anachronism. Perhaps the termination date for the Modern English period will be 1970, a convenient rounding off of 1957 with its first orbital space flight or 1969 with its first landing on another planet. Certainly either of these two events is unique in the history of the world, and the space age will undoubtedly influence future trends in historical linguistic study.[1]

Among the mileposts in the outer historical development of the English language, after England's period of Roman occupation ended in 410 A. D., the first important event was the Germanic invasion by tribes of Angles, Saxons, and Jutes in 449. In 597, Latin reentered the language through the missionary efforts of St. Augustine, and beginning with the first Danish invasion in 787, the infusion of Scandinavian languages helped to provide new vocabulary that included phonemes previously unknown in Anglo-Saxon. The centuries following the Norman Conquest in 1066 were a period of bilingualism in England, as French vocabulary, pronunciation, and spelling had a vast influence in shaping the revolutionized English language that emerged in the fourteenth century. Latin had its influence as it entered by way of French, and it had much influence in its own right during the Renaissance as scholars introduced "inkhorn terms" that have since become an integral part of the English language. To mention only one further historical event, the introduction of printing in 1475 had a most important effect on written English; not only did it supply examples by which the random spelling of words

---

[1]Future linguists, from a vantage point several centuries removed, might be able to work with phonetic change, but there are already identifiable trends resulting from Space Age English. Besides the introduction of new words (apogee and perigee, for example), the language has proved its adaptability by adding new definitions to existing words (such as umbilical) and liberally applying functional shift ("All systems are go").

could be standardized, but it marked the end of a period in which books were for only the favored few.[2]

Identifying these few among the many milestones of outer history has allowed the inner history of English to trace certain phonetic and grammatical trends, such as the first consonant shifts described in Grimm's Law and its exceptions as described by the second consonant shifts in Verner's Law, the Great English Vowel Shift, and the loss of inflections with its subsequent dependency on word order, which changed the synthetic language of Old English into the analytic language of Modern English. A concise, readily available source for tracing the major features of these inner changes is a good dictionary.

One important feature of a dictionary entry is to give the etymology, or history, of a word. A single word may have its own outer and inner history, its change in meaning and pronunciation through the years, but its given "derivation" usually refers to the earliest appearance of its root word in some ancient language. Philologist Mario Pei states that "the chroniclers of language are usually content to work their way back to Latin, Greek, or Anglo-Saxon and stop

---

[2]Margaret Bryant, *Modern English and Its Heritage*, 2nd ed. (New York: The Macmillan Co., 1962), p. 85. In Bryant's annotated list of important dates in the history of the English language (pp. 437-439), not only does she include events not standard in other lists, but she challenges the traditional dates of the three periods.

there."³ However, Latin, Greek, Anglo-Saxon (Old English), and many other languages were, at one time, all one language. There are no written records of that language, now called Indo-European, but it is assumed to have flourished about 5000 B. C. around the shores of the Baltic, now in modern Lithuania.⁴ When the Indo-European peoples began to migrate in different directions, lack of communication among the groups resulted in dialects, and then, in the course of centuries, the dialects evolved into entirely different languages--Sanskrit, Homeric Greek, early Latin, Celtic, and others.

Thus, when the etymology of a word indicates its origins in Anglo-Saxon or Latin, that is only the last part of its story. Pei goes further back in time, back to Indo-European as the original parent language, in order to show how a single Indo-European root word could have undergone such drastic changes in form and meaning as to have produced pairs of words whose relationship is now unsuspected. "Philology," he says, "makes strange bedfellows of our most common words."⁵

---

³Mario Pei, "Language's Curious Couples," Saturday Review, XLIII (December 3, 1960), 20. The three columns on this page give an excellent, succinct summary of the process by which scholars identify languages evolved from a single parent language, as well as an explanation of how scholars have gone about reconstructing much of the hypothetical Indo-European language.

⁴Ibid. These facts, detailed in many other sources, are summarized in Pei's article.

⁵Ibid., p. 63.

Briefly tracing etymologies, he finds a common root for baby and barbarian, as connected with babble; for judge and teach; for beetle and fission; and, among other pairs, for whiskey and biology. These curious linguistic couples, although they have their origins in a tongue that has been "dead" for some seven thousand years, suggest that "there's at least some life in the old language yet."[6]

As illustrated with the hypothetical history of the hypothetical Indo-European language, there is a point beyond which scholars must base their theories on speculation. Ancient historians such as Bede and the contributors to the Anglo-Saxon Chronicle have supplied valuable medieval historical records, but there are undoubtedly many historical events that would have helped linguists immensely if only they had been recorded. Just as the recording of historical events is dependent on the human element, so is change in language. To questions about why Anglo-Saxons began to simplify their complicated inflectional system or why, "during the period of the Great Vowel Shift, they tended toward that particular kind of diphthongization, there must be a human answer."[7] Although we can speculate upon the reasons for a word's being pronounced a certain way and then changing its pronunciation, history will preserve its secrets.

---

[6] Ibid.

[7] Anthony Burgess, Urgent Copy: Literary Studies (New York: Morton and Company, Inc., 1968), p. 221.

Throughout history, writers of fiction have been ingenious in selecting as settings those spaces in which history is silent, but writers in the field of fantasy literature have the added advantage of being able, without actually rearranging history, to create an "as if" situation. L. Sprague de Camp, a historian and phonetician, creates a "might have been" heritage for the English language in "Wheels of If."[8] He uses the literary device of parallel worlds, a theory that at the instant of some momentous decision in history, there are alternate worlds in abeyance, one of which will happen depending on what decision is made. The historical moment in this case is the Synod of Whitby in 664, when the Anglo-Saxon world had to choose between the leadership of the Celtic Christian Church and the Roman Christian Church. "Wheels of If" is set in twentieth-century America, but America as it would have been if the Anglo-Saxons had chosen to follow the leadership of the Celtic Christian Church, instead of the Roman.

The nontechnical reader will probably miss the significance of two short, seemingly unrelated episodes that preface the story. In the first, King Oswiu of Northumbria sits in the Synod of Whitby, in 664, bored by the proceedings and growing increasingly irritated by thoughts of his nagging wife Eanfled and his wary dislike of the bishop in charge. Disregarding

---

[8]Lyon Sprague De Camp, "Wheels of If," _Wheels of If and Other Science Fiction_ (New York: Shasta Publishers, Inc., 1948), pp.3-99.

the ecclesiastical and documentary evidence offered, King Oswiu impulsively makes his choice out of personal pique and defiance of the bishop. This is the incident, without comment from the author. A historian would be alerted by the presence of the Synod of Whitby, an event of actual history, and he would recognize that King Oswiu's choice was irrelevant to the purpose of the ecclesiastical conference. It is at this point that history shifts to fantasy, and failing to recognize the significance is to miss a vital basis of the entire story. The modern world, as well as the modern English language, is the result of many historical decisions, many of them as tenuous and arbitrary as King Oswiu's. Whims change the course of history, and the protagonist, Allistair Park, is given the chance to visit a "might have been" world.

Allistair Park of twentieth-century America wakes to find himself in another world, in a body of the same age and physique as his own, but he is wearing a cleric's collar and a large ring bearing a Celtic cross. Finding a newspaper, The New Belfast Sooth, he verifies the date and sees this article:

BISJAP STIL MISING

> At a laet aur jestrdai nee toocan had ben faund of yi mising Bisjap Ib Scoglund of yi Niu Belfast Bisjapric of yi Celtic Cristjan Tjörtj, hwuuz vanisjing a wiik agoo haz sterd yi börg. Cnicts sai yai aar leeving nee steen ontörnd in yaeir straif to faind yi hwarabauts of yi mising preetjr, hwuuz lösti swink on bihaaf of yi Screlingz haz bimikst him in a fiirs yingli scofal. . .[9]

---

[9]Ibid, p. 23.

The writing, he realizes, is English spelled phonetically according to the rules of his own language, with some Old and Middle English thrown in, and he translates:

> At a late hour yesterday no token (sign?) had been found of the missing Bishop Ib Scoglund of the New Belfast Bishopric of the Celtic Christian Church, whose vanishing a week ago has stirred the burg (city?). Cnicts (police?) say they are leaving no stone unturned in their strife (effort?) to find the whereabouts of the missing preacher.[10]

Eventually Park realizes that, somehow, he must be this "mising bisjap," and he locates the home of Ib Scoglund--his home now--and manages to conduct interviews with local "newsers" regarding his abduction and release. In the course of reinstating himself and becoming involved in a civil rights "scofal" concerning the Screlings (historical counterpart of the American Indian), Park is aided by his manservant, who supplies most of the conversational illustrations and serves as a link between the two worlds.

History, according to Bishop Ib Scoglund's "Wördbuk," was identical in Park's memory until the Dark Ages. Then he identifies the Synod of Whitby as the pivotal event, as King Oswiu had chosen to follow the Celtic Church, instead, and the Celtic form of Christianity had spread over Great Britain and Scandinavia. The dying Roman Church had sponsored one Crusade among the Franks, but it resulted in Arab retaliation that literally decimated the Franks and destroyed their

---

[10]Ibid., p. 24.

influence forever. In this world, the French did not invade England in 1066, nor did any other historical event subsequent to 664 happen exactly as it had in Park's world. By 664, the Germanic tribes had already invaded England, but the Danish occupation of England in this alternate world had been a relatively peaceful affair. A Danish king named Gorm had brought both the British Isles and Scandinavia under his rule and, more successful than Cnut had been, Gorm's reign had perpetuated the union between the two until the present time. North America had been discovered by a Danish explorer in 989 A. D. and colonized by Scandinavian tribes.[11] Park then realizes that this is the world that would have evolved if King Oswiu had made the alternate decision, and he is now in the body of the man he would have become had that world evolved. English is spoken as it would have been if the events of history had been different.

In this America with its five-century headstart over Christopher Columbus, the first Americans had escaped almost all of the events of outer history that had had a profound effect upon the evolution of Park's English language. Examination of the inner history of this "might have been" English language reveals, however, that at least some of its grammatical aspects developed in quite a parallel way.

Inflections have disappeared, with the exception of a

---

[11]Ibid, pp. 29-31.

few initial verbal inflections such as "<u>bimikst</u> in a scuffle" and "<u>bifreed</u> from captors." Apparently, the loss of inflections was inevitable. Loss of the Anglo-Saxon long vowels has begun, their value being represented by doubling the short vowel, as in <u>hwuuz</u>, <u>fiirs</u>, <u>toocan</u>, and <u>wiik</u>. Development is approximately six centuries late, according to Park, who has read Chaucer. Similarly, the Great Vowel Shift has lagged behind in fully developing its diphthongization, or perhaps the written words represent only a variation in spelling and not a phonetic difference.

Some words have taken an alternate path in their etymological development, as Park discovers, when he is told to "step on the strangle," meaning a throttle or a choke. Probably the most significant differences in the vocabulary of this imaginary language are those that would have been effected by the Norman invasion. There are virtually no Latin-derived words. Still retained is its Anglo-Saxon vocabulary, as is illustrated in the following list of Latin-by-way-of-French words that did <u>not</u> evolve:

```
börg--city
straif--effort
swink--toil, labor, work
sterd--excited
vanisjing--disappearance
newser--reporter
wördbuk--dictionary, encyclopedia
choosings--elections
ghostly--spiritual
```

Automobiles, when they were invented, were called "wains,"

and by the twentieth century, there are folkwains, goodwains, knickwains, and even airwains. The most etymologically interesting word, however, is cnict. Throughout history, knights had represented law enforcement, and so the word was eventually applied to the police, still retaining the pronunciation of the initial c, pronounced as [k]. By this time, slang has changed it to knick in speech, but other than the final phoneme, it is uncertain what spoken difference de Camp indicates between the spellings cnict and knick.

The Great Vowel Shift had gotten a slow start, but Grimm's Law was even slower. The Screlings hail from the Dhacoosja (Dakota) territory, and a battle takes place on the banks of the Okeeyo (Ohio) River. The voiced aspirated stop dh has not shifted to the voiced stop d, which represents the third and final stage, and neither has the voiceless stop k evolved into the voiceless fricative h, which is the first stage of the process. It seems that Grimm's Law has entirely bypassed Ib Scoglund's world.[12]

---

[12]De Camp's Dhacoosja and Okeeyo illustrate stages one and three described in Grimm's Law. Stage two is missing, and the sj in Dhacoosja is irrelevant to the consonants affected by Grimm's Law. It seems that de Camp could have made the series complete by saying "Dhacooda" instead of Dhacoosja, since the second stage would have involved the voiced stop d shifting to the voiceless stop t.

De Camp comments, however, that "Dhacoosja is a hypothetical spelling, not of Dakota, but of Dakotia, an imagined Amerind principality with a Romance termination tacked on. By normal phonetic development, the -tia would develop into some sort of [ʃə] or [çə]." (letter dated February 10, 1971)

Another obvious factor is spelling. This alphabet, also, has lost the Anglo-Saxon letters *ae* (digraph), *þ* (thorn), and *ð* (eth). The lack of the two latter ones must have prompted early printers, as it did Caxton, to use a *y* to represent *th*, but the substitution has become fixed in this alphabet. Old English *sc* (pronounced *sh*), as Park remembered, had taken on an additional pronunciation under Scandinavian influence, retaining its Old English sound initial in *ship* and taking on Danish initial sound in *sky*. In the imaginary language, Old English *sc* is spelled *sj*, as in *bisjap*, and Danish *sc* is either *sc* or *sk*; the Old English *c*, although it evolved into the same velar [ch], is represented by *tj*, as in *tjörtj*.

There is some attempt in the "Wheels of If" to indicate phonetics in the speech. Park's manservant calls the bishop a "*fickter* in the *fick* for the *ricks*" of the oppressed Screlings and says that "*thocks* of *hicker* things *ock*" to be good for him. Ib Scoglund is called a "kind-*lick*" man, and the servant replies, "*Rick-lick* (rightly) so." Even with these Anglo-Saxon remains fairly intact, Danish influence has been much stronger in this alternate world than in Park's world. Danish parliament is still called a *thing*, districts are still called *hides*, and the members are *thanes*. At a meeting of the Twoth Hide Thing, with Thinglitarian Beurwulf acting as chairman, a motion is "made and twoth."

In creating this imaginary "English as it might have

been" language, de Camp more than adequately demonstrates his knowledge of the historical development of English. A modern writer can hardly describe the language in its own terminology, so firmly have Latin and French become embedded into our present day English. A critic has commented that de Camp, a phonetician who has published in many scholarly journals, is primarily a writer of fiction. While he might prefer to write the speech of his characters in phonetic symbols, particularly with glottal and guttural sounds now lost to English, he knows where to draw the line for his non-technical readers.[13] Nevertheless, it would be interesting to see what de Camp could have done to the imaginary language if he had intended it to be read by adventurous scholars of Anglo-Saxon with a background in phonetics.

In addition to the unilluminated spots in history, another convenient sanctuary for writers of fantasy literature is the future. This device is a familiar one, particularly in utopian or anti-utopian fiction, as an author takes his stance in the distant future. From this vantage point, it can be illustrated how the world virtually destroyed itself during the twentieth century, leaving only a few survivors to exist through the (future) Dark Ages, begin a renaissance of some sort, and progress into that period of enlightenment

---

[13]Isaac Asimov, preface to de Camp's The Continent Makers (New York: Doubleday, Doran, and Company, 1954), pp. 11-14. See also de Camp's phonetic instructions to the reader, p. 15.

called the "present." The nature of those few survivors, whether good or bad, determines the nature of the future society and the genre of the book. This pattern of action allows an author to create future historical events to suit his own purposes, but it, like the pattern of preliminary action mentioned previously, is a convenient vehicle that may be discarded when the story begins.

One writer has created an imaginary future society by entirely omitting this preliminary pattern and reversing the usual procedure involved in historical linguistic analysis. Normally, the starting point is a historical event, from which linguists abstract their working materials. Anthony Burgess, in A Clockwork Orange, creates an imaginary language that forces linguistic analysis in order to deduce what historical events led to its development:

> Our pockets were full of deng, so there was no real need from the point of view of crasting any more pretty polly to tolchock some old veck in an alley and viddy him swim in his blood while we counted the takings and divided by four, nor to do the ultraviolet on some shivering starry grey-haired ptitsa in a shop and go smecking off with the till's guts.[14]

The entire book is a narrative written in a teenage jargon of the future, called Nadsat, "a weird argot that seems to be all its own. . .neither gibberish nor a Joycean exercise."[15]

---

[14]Anthony Burgess, A Clockwork Orange (New York: W. W. Norton and Company, Inc., 1963), p. 1.

[15]Time, LXXXI (February 15, 1963), 103.

Burgess begins by making it easy for the reader to fit strange words into context, such as wearing a wig on the "gulliver" or talking out of the corner of the "rot." Then he places more burden on the reader as Alex, the fifteen-year-old narrator, leads his three "droogs" into the delinquent adventures that begin the story. After several glasses of the typical teenager's drink, doped milk, Alex and his gang decided to break into someone's home, simply for something to do. Alex says,

> I knocked, and I could slooshy somebody coming, then
> I could viddy this one glaz looking out at me. . . .
> "Yes? Who is it?" It was a sharp's goloss, a youngish
> devotchka by her sound. . . .[16]

As Alex's "droogs" creep up "horrowshow stealthy" behind him, the four force their way into the house, where they find a "chelloveck" wearing "horn-rimmed otchkies" seated at a typewriter, working on the manuscript of a book called <u>A Clockwork Orange</u>. Alex reads "a malenky bit" of it aloud, telling the terrified writer, "Never fear. If fear thou hast in thy heart, O brother, pray banish it forthwith."[17]

Alex and his companions are hoodlums, and this socialistic future England is terrified by its teenagers, who rule the country by night. <u>A Clockwork Orange</u> has a story to tell, and a good one it is, but the most fascinating feature of the book is the language. It fluctuates from entirely alien terminology into oddly archaic diction, sometimes giving religious conno-

---

[16]<u>Ibid</u>., p. 19-20.   [17]<u>Ibid</u>., p. 21.

tation (". . .go all on his jeezny being as a little child. . . ."), and sometimes lapsing into baby talk (". . . mounching my toast dipped in jammiwam and eggiweg. . ."). Alex combs his "luscious glory" and counts "odin dva tree" as he waits for the "millicents" to arrest him. In prison, a psychiatrist remarks that this "dialect of the tribe" is quaint, and another doctor explains, "Odd bits of old rhyming slang. . . and a bit of gipsy talk, too. But most of the roots are Slav. Propaganda. Subliminal penetration."[18]

In this explanation, Burgess has given a hint about the historical roots of this language, or rather, this teenage jargon. The word <u>Nadsat</u> itself is the affix to the numerals eleven through nineteen in Russian, a word roughly equivalent to the English "teen." Critic Stanley Edgar Hyman says of the language, "Nadsat is not quite so hard to decipher as Cretan Linear B,"[19] but the ordinary reader automatically begins to compile a glossary as he collects words in context, without any idea of where the words originated. Anyone acquainted with Russian, however, would be able to connect "gulliver" with <u>golova</u>, "head" in Russian. One of Alex's favorite adjectives of praise is "horrowshow," which is a corruption of <u>khorosho</u>, Russian equivalent of "well, good." Russian <u>militsia</u>, or police, become "millicents." <u>Kopat</u>, "to dig with a shovel,"

---

[18]Ibid., p. 114.

[19]Ibid., p. 182. The first edition in hardback, published in 1962, had no help for the reader. This later paperback edition is especially valuable for its afterword by Hyman with his analysis of Nadsat and his dictionary of Nadsat words.

is used as "dig" in the slang sense of "enjoy, understand," and British "bird," slang meaning a girl, becomes ptitsa, its Russian equivalent.

This intermingling of English and Russian, in both the literal and the semantic sense, along with anglicized pronunciations, describes an English language that has settled down after the invasion of Russian language and Russian culture. The infusion of culture is reflected by the fact that almost all of the altered words denote every day actions and objects--man, woman, eat, drink, sleep, good, bad. Hyman estimates that at least three-quarters of the Nadsat language is Russian.[20]

The remaining quarter is composed of schoolboy slang, Cockney rhyming slang, remnants of baby talk, Biblical allusions and terminology, Shakespearean quotations, a pattern of double and triple negatives, and a syntactical sentence pattern identical to modern German.

The setting for A Clockwork Orange is the future, but nowhere in the book is there an indication of even the approximate date. A long passage of time is indicated, however, during Alex's imprisonment as he hears an older prisoner use "old-time criminal slang" that is unintelligible to the younger boy. A forecast of future language comes when Alex cannot understand several girls only a few years younger than he.

---

[20]Ibid., p. 181.

It would be possible to evaluate this book, and others similar to it, without linguistic analysis. The England in the story has, for some reason, lost its moral and ethical sense, its incentive for individual initiative, and its faith in God. It is a mechanical thing parading as organic, like a clockwork orange. But the literary analysis would be much more valuable if that reason could be identified. Linguistics supplies the information that the language is three-quarters Russianate, that the retained English elements are atypical of ordinary conversation, and that at its period of occurrence it is in an advanced stage of development. Therefore, this society must reflect the results of Russian occupation over a long period of time.

It is unlikely that many literary works could profit by the application of historical linguistics as a tool science in literary criticism. A Clockwork Orange does, and in a very different way, the knowledge of historical linguistics helps to convert "Wheels of If" from a piece of escape fiction into a linguistic work of art.

CHAPTER V

SPEAKING THE SAME LANGUAGE

Travel involves not only a change of locale, but a change of language, whether in regional dialects of the same language or into an entirely different language. Any difficulties encountered by a modern tourist would be insignificant when compared to the range of travel offered in science fiction--space ships to any remote planet in the galaxy and time travel to any past or future age. One common problem of all situations in which two languages meet, whether in reality or in fantasy, is finding some means to communicate, devising some way in which men can speak the same language.

To say that two people do not "speak the same language" might be taken figuratively or literally. No doubt, many marital arguments remain unresolved because husband and wife do not "speak the same language" about household finances or child rearing. Taken literally, communication within our multilingual world has always been a problem, and it is still a problem, despite phenomenal advances in other fields. Americans can go to the moon, but they cannot communicate that fact to other nations without polyglot interpreters as go-betweens, and to announce it to the whole world at once would require some three thousand interpreters.[1] The real problem is most obvious when a great many languages are represented in one group, such as the United Nations, in which each language requires a team of skilled interpreters to provide hours of continuous translation. To conduct such an assembly in one common language, to mention only a few advantages, would reduce the sheer number of persons involved, expedite the proceedings, and allow for personal exchanges between members. The idea of using a common language in such circumstances is commendable, but in actuality, it has proved not to be so simple.

One suggestion has been a type of international, artificial language, whose basis is a vocabulary and grammar composed of bits of existing spoken languages. Root words from Latin and Greek are used, with a few inflections common to several major modern European languages, but the predominating theory is "the greatest meaning to the greatest number." This type of artificial language utilizes base words whose general meaning is known to speakers of several languages (such as chron- and temp-, which have something to do with time), but as a deliberate creation, the language is entirely intelligible to no linguistic group. Perhaps the most widely known artificial language is Esperanto, but there have been no less than

---

[1]Jacob Ornstein and William W. Gage, The ABC's of Languages and Linguistics (New York: Chilton Publishers, 1964), p. 146.

six hundred such schemes proposed through the years--Interlingua, Novial, Interglossa, Ido, Volapük, Kosmos, Spokil, Universala, and Occidental, to mention only a few.[2] Most artificial languages are based on linguistic universality--common word forms and their meanings--but others have been based on other universal elements, or polygraphs, such as Solresol (based on the musical scale) and Symbology (allotting the number 6 to indicate a tree and 8 to indicate a house, for example.)[3] Although most of the artificial languages suggested are adequate for the purpose, such systems have inherent disadvantages. For one thing, a majority of them have been designed by and for Western Europeans and essentially retain their Indo-European characters. Speakers of Oriental languages find them every bit as difficult to learn as any Western language. A second problem lies in the phonetic system. While an adult may learn to recognize written symbols and train himself in a foreign grammatical structure, he cannot always learn to make sounds entirely foreign to his native tongue. All attempts to create an acceptable artificial world language have failed, perhaps because in all the languages of the world with their diverse linguistic arrangements, to find a common denominator in form-classes or phonetics or thought patterns would be an impossible task. Today, advocating the use of an artificial

---

[2] Ibid.

[3] Ibid., p. 153.

language represents more of an idealistic movement than a practical solution.[4]

A second type of suggested world language involves the use of an actual language, simplified in structure and reduced in vocabulary for ease in learning. The first efforts were in reviving Latin and simplifying that "dead language" by removing its complicated inflectional system.[5] Then modern languages--English, for example--were suggested as a basis for a world language, with modifications and simplifications adapted to basic communication among speakers of existing languages. The best known of this type of Basic English is that devised by C. K. Ogden and promoted by I. A. Richards.[6] Ogden-Richards Basic English is not a reorganization of the English language, but a simplification. Sentence structure remains unaltered, although simple, declarative sentences seem most suitable. With a reduced vocabulary of only 850 words, it contains words in all the existing parts of speech, but it utilizes eighteen special auxiliary verbs, or "operators," such as _get_, _do_, _take_, and _make_ to form verbal phrases and drastically reduce the

---

[4]Robert A. Hall, Jr., _Linguistics and Your Language_ (Garden City, New York: Doubleday and Company, Inc., 1960), p. 233.

[5]Mario Pei, _One Language for the World: And How to Achieve It_ (New York: The Devin-Adair Company, 1961), pp. 124-26.

[6]I. A. Richards, _So Much Nearer_. Chapter 10 is a detailed summary of the principles of Ogden-Richards Basic English, although the theme of this book is computer instruction in public education.

number of verbs.

This basic language has a small total number of words, but words may be put together in different ways to say almost anything which a general-purpose language has to take care of. This basic language is not very good for writing poetry or literature because its list of words is short and it has not the ability to express emotions of the heart and soul. But there is nothing in good Basic which goes against the rules of good English. It has enough words and enough variety of word combinations to make adequate understanding possible when men want to discuss ideas which they hold in common. All its sounds may be put on one recording, and teaching the language with the help of sound motion pictures can be simple. To use this language for world communication is possible; this paragraph is written in Ogden-Richards Basic English.

Although this particular Basic English system is practicable, and the necessity of using slightly awkward phrases and overusing key words would be irritating only to a native speaker of English, critics have pointed out that Richards has made no provisions for the phonetic side of the problem. Within its small vocabulary are found all the phonemes in the English language, and so it must be intended only as a written auxiliary language. However, the selection of this or any other existing language for world communication has been unacceptable for several reasons. One problem is that the person who learns the 850 words will not stop at that point.

Each language carries its cultural and partisan feelings, and English-speakers do not want Basic Russian as a world language any more than Russians want Basic English or Basic Arabic or Basic Mandarin Chinese.[7]

It is ironic that the most successful interlanguage, a minimal language called "pidgin," reflecting the Chinese pronunciation of "business," evolved of itself without premeditation or scholarly guidance. Varieties of Pidgin English are spoken in China, West Africa, Melanesia, and Australia, among other places, and although each is a language with a linguistic structure of its own, a pidgin is indigenous to a specific bilingual or trilingual area. As such, any pidgin has narrow limitations and, like trade languages, would not be adequate for universal usage.[8]

Fantasy is not so different from reality. Writers of fantasy literature also create artificial and basic languages, but the only difference between their creations and those of men like Ludwik Zamenhof (creator of Esperanto) and I. A. Richards is that the fictional languages work. A writer of

---

[7] Throughout One Language for the World, Pei seems to favor the uninflected, isolating form of Chinese as a pattern for constructing an artificial language.

[8] Hall, pp. 234-36. (Pei, although admitting the usefulness of pidgin languages and trade languages like Swahili, calls them "baby talk that is no substitute for a true language." See One Language, pp. 56 and 79.) Hall has written the entry on pidgin for Compton's Encyclopedia (1969 edition) and Encyclopedia Britannica (1967 edition), in addition to the items listed in the bibliography. See also Hockett, A Course in Modern Linguistics, pp. 420-424.

fiction can be assured of it because he also creates the people who speak it, the reason for its presence in the fictional society, and quite often, the fictional originator of the altered language. Obviously the most suitable type for an author to use in his book is a version of Basic English, inasmuch as he is writing for English readers whose intellect he does not want to tax unduly with another Esperanto or "lingua mundo."

Undoubtedly, the best known fictional Basic English is Newspeak, a deliberately created and controlled language spoken by the citizens of a future England in George Orwell's 1984. Newspeak is a political tool, and its presence is such an integral factor in the book that an appendix, "The Principles of Newspeak," is included as part of the text. As explained in the appendix, Newspeak is divided into three distinct vocabulary classes known as the A vocabulary, the B vocabulary, and the C vocabulary. The latter consists entirely of scientific and technical terms and is of no interest to the layman. The B vocabulary is composed of compound words created specifically for their political importance, an issue which will be more cogent to a later chapter of this study. Within the section concerning the A vocabulary,[9] those words needed commonly for the business of everyday life, is an analysis of the rules upon which the language is constructed and which

---

[9] George Orwell, 1984 (New York: Harcourt, Brace and Company, 1949), pp. 247-49.

generally define the grammatical objectives of all basic languages, both fictional and actual. The two most important goals of a basic language are reduction of vocabulary and regularity of grammatical parts. Newspeak, operating within the context of *1984*, begins the first goal by eliminating words that are politically objectionable, but the remainder of the process is entirely linguistic.

There is, first, almost complete interchangeability between different parts of speech. A single word may serve as noun, verb, adjective, or adverb without altering its form. A second reduction is possible by assigning one clear-cut word for common usage and eliminating all possible synonyms. Further reduction involves the elimination of antonyms by selecting either of the pair (either *good* or *bad*, for example) and using the prefix *-un* to negate it. Adjectives are formed by adding *-ful* and adverbs by adding *-wise*; degrees of intensification are formed by adding *plus-* or, for greater emphasis, *doubleplus-*. Thus a single word, like *good*, can be used to serve a variety of functions:

```
            good
           ungood
         plusungood
       doubleplusungood
          plusgood
       doubleplusgood
           goodwise
```

The second feature of Newspeak, that of grammatical regularity, involves mostly nouns and verbs. The plural of all nouns is formed by adding -s to the singular form--mans, childs, lifes. Irregular verb forms are eliminated by adding the suffix -ed to form all past tenses--eated, drinked, bringed. Other than the standardization involving nouns and verbs, only the comparative degrees of adjectives and adverbs need attention. Both add -er and -est (good, gooder, goodest; ungood, ungooder, ungoodest), except when the resulting word is difficult to pronounce or is likely to be heard incorrectly. A sentence such as "The mans speaked doubleplusungoodwise" would be correct in Newspeak.

In composing this fictional Basic English (a feat which is most phenomenal in the B vocabulary with its political words), Orwell's thoroughness is remiss on only one point which is not clarified in the appendix nor in the conversation of characters. The verb to be, a maverick in most verbal systems, is not given special attention. However, characters in the book do not speak Newspeak outside of a few unusually significant words. Orwell, as a realist, sees national adoption of such a language as a gradual process, and Big Brother's linguists and lexicographers have projected the year 2050 for total usage of Newspeak and total obsolescence of Oldspeak, or standard English.

Orwell so thoroughly analyzes Newspeak in the appendix that grammarians have little to add. Such thoroughness in describing an entire language system is rare in fiction, however, and most writers either describe or illustrate only portions of their created language. Aliens in science fiction often speak a modified form of English, such as saying, "Do negatively self-preoccupy" to mean "Don't worry about it."[10] The use of a few phrases of this sort is not usually important, but it does reenforce the general theme of fantasy.

An incidental reference in L. Sprague de Camp's "New Arcadia" indicates to the reader that conversation is taking place in an interplanetary pidgin called Intermundos. The protagonist is an interplanetary reporter, and Intermundos is a pidgin designed out of "exobiological" consideration of the several species who speak it. Native languages among the extraterrestrial species have only seven consonants and three vowels in common, and Intermundos uses only these ten phonemes with a structure based mainly on terran tongues. As the narrator describes it,

> It was developed to be speakable by different species; hence it is phonetically simple . . . . It allows for variation in pronunciation: thus the s̱ may stand for any voiceless fricative like f̱ and ḥ; ṉ may be any nasal, and so on. (At that, it gives trouble to some species like the Serians who can't make nasal sounds.) . . . Having a rigid word order, it is good only for bare statements, as in any natural language. I called: "Ula las Sinvlianu! Na aki sal ain knaavu vun saaiṣu vun vuus?" meaning "Cimbrians! Where is your chief?"[11]

---

[10]Bruce McAllister, "The Faces Outside," 9th Annual Edition: The Year's Best S-F, Judith Merril, ed. (New York: Dell Publishing Co., 1964), p. 114.

[11]L. Sprague de Camp, "New Arcadia," A Gun for Dinosaur (New York: Doubleday and Company, Inc., 1963), p. 339.

The Intermundos sentence is obviously longer, but the presence of only this one phrase does not allow extensive testing of de Camp's phonetic theory. Only two words correlate with certainty:

>Sinvlianu
>Cimbrians

In addition to other phonetic variables, an exolinguist can assume that _l_ may also stand for _r_ and that _-u_ is a noun-pronoun suffix. There are three such words—<u>Sinvlianu</u>, <u>knaavu</u>, and <u>saaisu</u>—the first two being plural and the third singular. Therefore, there must be another structure signal to indicate number, but no definite signal occurs to form a pattern. Asked about his construction of Intermundos, de Camp said:

>I wrote THE WHEELS OF IF and NEW ARCADIA quite some time ago: in 1940 and 1955 respectively, so I can't be too sure of what I had in mind at the time.
>   As I recall, the final _-u_ in the Intermundos sentence was a sign, not of the plural, but of the noun. The nouns are not inflected for number, but number is indicated by the article. The word-for-word translation of the sentence would be: <u>Ula</u> (=French <u>hola</u>); <u>las</u> (=Spanish pl. def. art.); <u>Sinvlianu</u> (=Cimbrians); <u>Na</u> (the Chinese interrogative particle); <u>aki</u> (=Spanish <u>aqui</u>); <u>sal</u> (=Spanish <u>ser</u>); <u>ain</u> (=German <u>ein</u>); <u>knaavu</u> (not sure, but I think it may have something to do with German <u>Knabe</u>); <u>vun</u> (=German <u>von</u>); <u>saaisu</u> (this one baffles me; Caesar? sheikh?); <u>vuus</u> (=French <u>vous</u>). The _l_ may stand for either _l_ or _r_.
>. . . . .
>   Maybe <u>saaisu</u> means "size," although in that case I ought to have made it <u>saaizu</u>. Or maybe not. I had a phonetic scheme all worked out at the time, but I haven't

preserved it and don't recall it sixteen years later.[12]

Intermundos has absolutely no function in this story. Its presence illustrates nothing more than the author's love of language and theoretical phonetics.[13] "Fictionalized shoptalk" is an apt description of many of de Camp's writings, as well as of "Barrier,"[14] a long short-story written by Anthony Boucher that brings together some of the most improbable games that can be played with the English language.

"Barrier" is a linguist's carnival! Time travel is the device, but language is the overriding theme and the primary source of comedy. John Brent, of 1942, is selected for a mission of future historical study, one of the qualifications being his linguistic adaptability. Because no one know the nature of the language to be spoken in the twenty-fifth century, his destination, Brent has been tested on his ability to assimilate the principles of several fictitious languages invented for the purpose. When he lands in the year 2473 and

---

[12]Letter dated February 10, 1971. In a later letter (February 18, 1971), de Camp makes this emendation: "After I wrote it, I recalled that the Chinese interrogative particle is ni, not na . . . ."

[13]De Camp is a prolific writer of both fiction and nonfiction. His knowledge of history and phonetics appears in other fiction works pertaining to other periods of history and other languages. The Continent Makers contains stories in which Brazil has become the dominant world power and Portuguese the major linguistic influence.

[14]Anthony Boucher, "Barrier," Spectrum 4, Kingsley Amis, ed. (New York: Berkley Publishing Corporation, 1959).

asks the first passer-by, "What city is this?" he is answered, "Stappers will get you. Or be you Slanduch?"[15] Stappers, he learns, are the police, and they will "get" him because he has said is. (He fortunately chooses to say he is "Slanduch," and later finds that the Slanduch are notoriously careless with their grammar, being the only polyglot people left in existence, and are excused for occasional solecisms.)

The stranger says, "That bees O. K. Stappers be more severe now since Edict of 2470. Before they doed pardon some irregularities, but now none even from Slanduch."[16] With this first encounter, Brent begins registering the principles that he must apply in speech: omit all articles, end all past tense verbs with -ed and all third-person singulars with -s, pronounce does as "dooze," and say mans and womans and childs. Thereafter, Brent operates on a stolen identity card as a German Slanduch, a name whose origin is from Auslandeutsch, just as Stappers came from Gestapo. The language spoken is a type of Basic English from which all irregularities and non-essentials have been eliminated.

By 2473, every science has been analyzed, standardized, and frozen in its state of perfection, a linguist named Farthing having published his treatise "This Bees Speech" as a linguistic model to be followed by all citizens. Only four

---

[15]Ibid., p. 134
[16]Ibid.

world languages have survived--English, German, Russian, and Spanish--and each has followed the same pattern of standardization.[17] The breaking of a single grammatical rule is considered a subversive action. Brent nervously feels his way into the speech as, with a young scientist and his sister Martha, he discovers himself among a group of revolutionaries. Once, finding that her room has been searched, Martha asks, "Who haves beed here today?" and Brent answers, "I didn't . . . er, doedn't . . . er, I beed not here." Brent becomes involved in the action when he learns that the State, as a scientific measure to preserve stasis, has set up an electronic barrier to prevent both space and time travel. He has entered because the barrier is effective only toward the future, and he entered from the past.

Alcoholic drinks are forbidden, but Brent's revolutionary friends keep "bond" on hand. Brent's journal includes items of linguistic interest, and so he asks why all alcohol is called bond. Martha tells him,

> When they prohibited all drinking because drinking makes you think world bees better than it really bees and of course if you make yourself different world that bees against Stasis and so they prohibited it but they keeped on using it for medical purposes and that beed in warehouses and pretty soon no one knowed any other kind of liquor so it bees called bond.[18]

---

[17]Ibid., p. 141. The next few pages include over four centuries of future history, including future historical linguistics.

[18]Ibid., p. 151.

Brent remarks on the "immortal spirit of Gracie Allen."

Because of his linguistic ability and his slight acquaintance with German, Brent is chosen to attend the dedication of the new, strengthened barrier as a Slanduch representative. When he and his friends, with explosives under their coats, are stopped and asked for credentials, the guard grins at Brent and says, "Also! Sie wesen Slandsdeutsch und zwar aus Deutschland! . . . . Seit jahre habe ich kein Wort deutsch gehört. Mein eltere wesen von deutsch kerkunft." Registering this similarly standardized German with <u>eltere</u> instead of <u>eltern</u> and the infinitive <u>wesen</u> and the omission of articles, Brent replies, "Freut mich sehr. Aber jetst habe ich kein zeit. Ich müsse eilen. Später vielleicht könne ich--Ach! Mein freunde wesen schön gegeht. Verzeihen sie!"[19] He escapes further conversation with the talkative Stapper, but makes a mental note to record this Basic German in his journal.

Their successful sabotage of the barrier does not end the story, because the barrier does not explode. Instead, it implodes, and the force of the implosion draws in every time and space traveler who has ever--rather, who will in the future ever--attempt to pass the barrier. They all land in one chaotic, wriggling heap, humans of all descriptions in all states of dress scrambling madly away from equally frightened

---

[19]Ibid., p. 160. <u>Kerkunft</u> is probably a misprint of <u>herkunft</u>.

antennaed, tenacled, scaled, and indescribable non-human creatures. Some hectic hours later, after Stappers have all of the time travelers in custody, Brent's services as a Slanduch interpreter are required. State Linguists are those who only know Farthing's grammatical rules by heart, and to communicate with the time travelers has been completely beyond them. Conducted into the language headquarters, Brent sees three of the time travelers he is to question--a bearded man in Elizabethan costume, a strapping Amazonic blonde, and one pale green, scaled, gilled biped. A frustrated state linguist tells Brent what information is required, and a Stapper with drawn gun reenforces the order.

Beginning with the Elizabethan, Brent asks,

> "O. K. You! . . . What part of time do you come from?"
> "A pox o' thee, sirrah, and the goodyears take thee! An thou wouldst but hearken to me, thou might'st learn all."
> The State linguist moaned. "You hear, young man? How can one interpret such jargon?"
> Brent smiled. "It bees O.K. This bees simply English as it beed speaked thousand years ago. This man must have beed aiming at earlier time and prepared himself. . . . Thy pardon, sir. These kerns deem all speech barbaric save that which their own conceit hath evolved. Bear with me, and all will be well."[20]

The bearded man, who longs to study Elizabethan England, has indeed prepared himself by learning sixteenth century English and dressing the part, and he repeatedly insists that he "would to the Mermaid Tavern."

The Amazon strides forth next, as Brent asks,

---

[20] Ibid., p. 166.

"Madam, what part of time do you come from?"
"Evyvuy taws so fuy," she growled. "Bu I unnasta. Wy cachoo unnasta me?"
Brent laughed. "Is that all that's the trouble? You don't mind if I go on talking like this, do you?"
"Naw. You taw howeh you wanna, slonsoo donna like I dih taw stray."
Fascinating, Brent thought. All final consonants lost, and many others. Vowels corrupted along lines indicated in twentieth-century colloquial speech. Consonants sometimes restored in liaison as in French. "What time do you come from then? . . . And your intentions here?"
"Twenny-ni twenny-fie. . . . Ai gonno intenchuns. Juh wanna see wha go."[21]

Bracing himself, Brent then approaches the green-skinned biped and asks where he comes from. The biped replies,

"Ya studier langue earthly. Vyerit todo langue isos. Ou comprendo wie govorit people."
Brent was on the ropes and groggy. The familiarity of some of the words made the entire speech even more incomprehensible. "Says which?" he gasped.
The green man exploded. "Ou existier nada but dolts, cochons, duraki v this terre? Nikovo parla langue earthly? Potztausend Sapperment en la leche de tu madre and I do mean you!"
Brent reeled. But even reeling he saw the disapproving frown of the State lingust and the itching fingers of the Stappers. He faced the green man calmly and said with utmost courtesy, "Twas brillig and the slithy toves did gyre and gimble over the rivering waters of the hitherandthithering waters of pigeons on the grass alas. Thank you, sir." He turned to the linguist. "He says he won't talk."[22]

Assimilating the random words of the green man in Russian and German and English, even the swearing in Spanish, Brent realizes that this polyglot "langue earthly" must be the result

---

[21]Ibid., p. 167.

[22]Ibid., pp. 167-68.

of an interplanetary mistake in assuming that there is one earthly language, just as we assume that there is a single Martian or a Venusian language. Because Brent is the only person who can speak with these time travelers, they are all released in his custody so that he can gather more information from them. Soon they discover that this mélange of languages allows them to speak in front of linguists and Stappers with perfect safety, and they make plans to overthrow the State and foster a new renaissance. Because they can speak the same language, they save the world.

Among the approaches to literary criticism, the one least mentioned and most needed with fantasy fiction is that of appreciation, a simple sense of enjoyment. "Barrier," read with the principles of linguistics as a springboard, is a delightful comedy. But the comic element is not in the plot; it is in the languages, both their grammatical systems and the difficulties they cause among the characters. It is not too far-fetched to imagine similar difficulties arising among speakers who attempt to communicate in an artificial, basic language with its range of expression and its vocabulary so much less versatile than a natural language. Even if such an auxiliary language were developed and accepted for use in international situations, it would probably be a relief for the speakers to return to their own native language in order to communicate with all the innuendoes and connotations and cultural associations that have accumulated over a lifetime.

CHAPTER VI

LEXICOGRAPHY AND "DOCTORED DICTIONARIES"

"One dictionary is as good as another to most people, who use them for spellers and bet-settlers and accessories to crossword puzzles and Scrabble games,"[1] and it would probably surprise many people to find that "the dictionary" does not exist. That is, there is no <u>one</u> dictionary, but many dictionaries whose information on a given entry may or may not agree. The existence of many dictionaries presupposes the existence of many dictionary makers, or lexicographers, and it is only recently that the men behind these modern monumental works have been called to public attention. Formerly, public attention was focused more on the authority of their product, the lexicon, and "almost the only individual to approach the sacred book in the spirit of doubter was the lexicographer himself."[2] The decade of the 1960's has seen a shift of

---

[1] Kurt Vonnegut, Jr., "The Dictionary," <u>Welcome to the Monkey House</u> (New York: Dell Publishing Co., Inc., 1968), p.112.

[2] Ernest Weekley, "On Dictionaries," <u>Dictionaries and That Dictionary</u>, James H. Sledd and Wilma R. Ebbitt, eds. (Chicago: Scott, Foresman and Co., 1962), p. 10. Also printed in <u>The Atlantic Monthly</u> (June 1924), pp. 782-91. Part I of Sledd and Ebbitt's anthology contains seven essays that provide an introduction to the history and scope of English lexicography.

critical attention, from the book itself to the procedure by which it was made, from dictionaries to dictionary-making.

The presence and use of a dictionary in a fantasy story would probably have little interest unless it gave information both unexpected and unusual. Assuming the integrity of even fictional lexicographers, such erroneous (known only to the reader) information must have been recorded as fact in their fictional dictionaries because the lexicographers believed it to be fact. Fictional dictionary makers follow the same process of compiling information that modern dictionary makers do, but the vehicle of make-believe allows an author to juggle their working materials. Besides providing comic value to the story, the resulting fictional definitions provoke thoughtful speculation when the reader realizes how many steps are involved in this intricate process and how easily misinformation can be perpetuated, and perhaps may have been, throughout history.

English lexicography had its beginnings in "glosses," or vocabulary lists defining "hard words" for the benefit of grammar school boys, the earliest being Robert Cawdry's The Table Alphabeticall of Hard Words, 1604. English was unworthy of the attention of medieval scholars, but with the advent of printing, cultured Elizabethans discovered a wonderful new heritage in their native language, and the idea leading to modern English lexicography was born. Versions of vocabulary lists of "hard words" in Latin and Greek existed in ancient times, but through Cawdry and his successors, similar words lists in English began to take on characteristics in form and content that have resulted in modern dictionaries. Modern lexicographers, with their improved technical and linguistic methods, have identified a good many etymological errors and myths due to misprints and inaccurate recording by early lexicographers,[3] but the early works have helped to preserve many now-obsolete words that would have otherwise been lost.

A study of the milestones in the history of lexicography will yield the names of many dedicated men who provided "firsts"--the first to alphabetize entries, the first to include "easy words," the first to provide biographical data, and, among others, the first to distinguish American English from British English.[4] Especially pertinent to this study is Samuel Johnson's famous A Dictionary of the English Language, 1755, not because of its many firsts collected under one cover, but because it was the harbinger of the modern usage movement.

Scholars of the Early Modern English period, primarily

---

[3]Ibid. Pages 10-21 contain a brief summary of the early history of lexicography.

[4]Several good histories of lexicography are listed in the bibliography. See also Joseph H. Friend, The Development of American Lexicography (The Hague, Netherlands: Manton and Co., Printers, 1967), pp. 24-34, for a summary of early British lexicography. Emphasis is on American lexicography, but this book is especially valuable for its facsimile pages of many out-of-date editions.

those during the Age of Reason, were prescriptivists. Whether the issue was writing poetry or criticizing a play or defining a word, they set down rules to be followed. Dictionary makers regarded their task as one of legislating how words should be pronounced and what they should mean. Samuel Johnson's prodigious attempt to define every important word in the English language, even though including some subjectively humorous or sardonic definitions, was the first dictionary to illustrate a defined word in context, through quotations as it was currently used by educated men. This observation is not to say that Dr. Johnson was an advocate of usage as the sole arbiter of definition; to the contrary, he was authoritarian and legislative, often condemning words as "low" or "ludicrous" and even ruling some obsolete.[5] Still, in providing examples of current usage, he set in motion what lexicography was to become more than two centuries later.

Modern lexicography recognizes that the duty of a lexicographer is to record usage, not to criticize or legislate. A word means whatever the speakers of the language deem it to mean, and a modern lexicographer defines a word only after he has first gathered examples of the word in common speech--not only in the speech of educated and cultured people, but in that of the uneducated and even illiterate. He may note that a word is used mainly by uneducated speakers or that it is

---

[5]Weekley, p. 16.

generally unacceptable in certain circles, but modern lexicography neither condemns or recommends--it merely records.[6]

The usage movement, as it has been stated earlier, is a very recent development, so new in the area of lexicography that the general American public is only now becoming aware of certain changes in technique. No doubt, the appearance of Webster's Third New International Dictionary in 1961 will be a major, if stormy, milestone in lexicographical history.[7] The furor is basically the result of misunderstanding, however, as even educated critics assume that this dictionary is sanctioning the use of ain't instead of simply recording the fact that some educated Americans do use the word in expressions such as "Ain't it the truth?" and "Ain't I?" Critics are reading as prescription what is intended only as description. This divergence between prescriptive and descriptive

---

[6]See Mario Pei, "A Loss for Words," Saturday Review, XLVII (November 14, 1964), 82-4. After summarizing the prescriptive-descriptive trend, Pei advocates a return to at least some measure of prescriptivism. Through advertizing slogans and dictionaries' refusals to give direction to those who honestly want to know "the best way to say it," he says, substandard usage is fast becoming the accepted standard. Pei's suggestion is that standard usage could just as easily be measured by the speech of cultured speakers in order to provide some grammatical guidelines. "Why not control language? he says (p. 83). "Why must it be allowed to lead a life of no restraints, when nobody and nothing else does?"

[7]Sledd and Ebbitt's Dictionaries and That Dictionary, pp. 50-248, is a gathering of sixty-two articles collected from various publications that reflect the reception of Webster's Third, with such titles as "Good English Ain't What We Thought" (pp. 80-82), "Webster's Way Out Dictionary" (p. 57), and "Finalized?" (p. 102).

attitudes is not uncommon. Critics in question undoubtedly received their education from prescriptive grammar books, just as today's older teachers prefer to apply the same prescriptive method of grammatical "do's and don't's" to school children who are, nevertheless, part of today's descriptive society.[8] The inclusion of the controversial, recently-coined verb finalize in Webster's Third reflects the fact that the word is already being used in speech, no matter what its age, and later editions of this and other dictionaries will undoubtedly include additional new words that fill a specific void in our language.[9] As one critic expresses it, "Homo Americanus is going to go on speaking and writing the way he always has, no matter what dictionary he owns."[10]

Dictionaries and dictionary making, as they occasionally

---

[8]Thomas Pyles, "Dictionaries and Usage," Linguistics Today, Archibald A. Hill, ed. (New York: Basic Books, Inc., 1969), p. 28. This "linguistic attitude gap" is effectively demonstrated by astute advertising methods on the part of Winston cigarettes. For years, singing television commercials have said, "Winston tastes good, like a cigarette should." A nation full of prescriptive-minded consumers evidently impressed Winston's advertisers that like should not be used as a conjunctive adverb--it should be ". . . as a cigarette should"! The new slogan, appearing in late 1970, added, "What do you want, good grammar or good taste?"

[9]For example, since Webster's Third in 1961, television newscasters have added the noun vietnamization, meaning the process of gradually returning to Viet Namese control those areas left unprotected with the withdrawal of American occupation troops. Curiously, a verb to vietnamize has not materialized.

[10]Vonnegut, p. 115.

appear in fictional literature, seem to utilize only one function of a lexical entry. A dictionary entry gives many types of information--etymology, derivation, alternate spellings, pronunciation, syllabication, dialect variants, synonym and antonyms--but the function most adaptable to fiction is that of definition. It is adaptable for several reasons, the most obvious being that it is more interesting to see a word defined differently than spelled differently. The <u>Newspeak Dictionary</u> in <u>1984</u> contains only redefined words, but its compilation does not fall within the area of true lexicography. It is not a description, but a mandate, and its compilers are neologists rather than lexicographers. Their sole duty is to invent new words, eliminate existing words, and publish the results as a list of the only words acceptable in national speech. In no way does this resemble modern dictionary making or reflect the idea of defining a word according to the way it is already used in common speech.

For a modern lexicographer to define a word through current usage is actually quite a complicated process, inasmuch as most "usage" is not staged for his benefit. "Usage" means simply the way people talk and write. In any spot in the nation (or in any other English-speaking nation), any given word might occur in a telephone conversation, at a cocktail party, on a television interview, or even in a State of the Union speech, but the task of the lexicographer (and his staff of hundreds) is to observe and record the word or expression in its context, for later examination. It is this most significant aspect of "written versus oral" usage that authors of fiction can utilize best. Modern lexicographers gather much of their material from printed matter, as well as conversation, but fictional lexicographers are given only written records to work with. Invariably, they are attempting to define through context some word or idea that they truly do not understand, which was lost during the period of dark ages following the near destruction of the world. They must rely on ancient documents (usually from the twentieth century), and the author has full control over what documents have survived.

Among the surviving documents in Robert Graves's Watch the Northwind Rise[11] are fragments of ancient twentieth-century dictionaries, books of poetry, and other unidentified writing, through which the scholars of Classical English have attempted to reconstruct that "dead" language. In this future utopia modeled after classical Greek society, poets are the rulers and legislators; the protagonist, Edward Venn-Thomas of the twentieth century is evoked into New Crete because of his most famous poem--which he has not yet written at the time of his evocation. Upon his arrival through time, he is first greeted by a man who says,

---

[11] Robert Graves, Watch the Northwind Rise (New York: Farrar, Straus and Cudahy, Inc., 1949).

>I am an authority on English. . . . I hope that you will pardon us for having brought you so far, i.e., so many generations ahead of your epoch. . . . Do I speak with correctitude? . . . Did I not make myself clear, viz., that I am a student of European languages of the Late Christian epoch and an authority on the English language? . . . No, we have summoned you from the living. The dead are, nem. con., dead. You have still some years to live.¹²

This man and his scholarly colleagues, who are curators of the surviving Late English texts, might be said to "speak lexicon," since the Latin abbreviations have as much meaning to them as any English words. Their conversation throughout the book contains these lexical abbreviations, and they take every opportunity to question the protagonist, an authentic twentieth-century speaker of Ancient English, about items in the compilation of their English Dictionary. (They speak English with Venn-Thomas, but the language of New Crete is based on Catalan, a language Venn-Thomas had conveniently learned from his Catalonian mother.)

The most heated scholarly debate, at the time of Venn-Thomas's arrival, concerns the transcriptions of certain verses in the "Liverpool find of Christmas cards," such as:

>Just to hope the day keeps fine
>For you and yours this Christmastime,

and:

>I hope this stocking's in your line
>When stars shine bright at Christmastime.¹³

---

¹²Ibid., pp. 7-8.

¹³Ibid., p. 8.

Attempting to explain the off-rhyme, the scholars argue whether "Christmastime" is or is not a dialect variant of the older "Christmastide" in this satire on typical scholarly debates.

History has also had to be reconstructed through the fragments of Late English texts. Many blank periods remain, but the scholars know Henry Tudor to have been "a witty court poet," and the cause of world holocaust had been an unidentified substance called "bright AIRAR from heaven" (an acronym which Venn-Thomas can identify as Artifically Induced Radio Active Rain). A summary of events is called a pravda, a word of obscure origin.[14]

The role played by these linguists and lexicographers in Watch the Northwind Rise is inconsequential to the plot, but their "lexicon speech" provides good comedy. Tired of being imposed upon, Venn-Thomas's final comment to them is, ". . . Right again, i.e., e.g., nem. con., and verb.sap., I'm not going back . . . on any condition."[15]

The documents allowed to survive in Walter M. Miller, Jr.'s A Canticle for Leibowitz[16] not only are of a different nature, but are an integral factor in the story. The fragments, many of which are unintelligible, are carefully preserved through the future dark ages, are instrumental in fostering a renaissance, and, in later centuries, are recorded microfilm. World

---

[14] Ibid., p. 40.

[15] Ibid., p. 245.

[16] Walter M. Miller, Jr., A Canticle for Leibowitz (New York: J. B. Lippincott Company, 1959).

destruction in this book was atomic, called the Flame Deluge, and the repentant physicist who had helped develop the atomic bomb, Isaac Leibowitz, is now a candidate for canonization. In the months immediately following the initial atomic blast with its radioactive fallout, a group advocating simplification of life (including a return to illiteracy) had begun systematically destroying all printed matter. Leibowitz then became a "booklegger," collecting and secreting for posterity whatever writing he could find, and it is for this reason that he is under consideration for canonization. Every few centuries a new cache would be discovered and added to the existing collection, now called the Memorabilia. The New Roman Catholic Church has survived into this future dark age, having preserved the Memorabilia by recopying the items (with questionable accuracy) every few centuries, and it is through these recorded items--scraps of newspapers and magazines, random pages from novels and scientific treatises--that certain words in Pre-Deluge English have been defined.

The story begins in the desert as the bumbling but devout novice, Brother Francis, accidentally stumbles into an ancient fallout shelter. He is terrified, never having seen a Fallout, but knowing it to be a Deluge-spawned monster that "fell on the land and destroyed," as well as despoiling virgins in their sleep; the multitudes of misshapen and ill-begotten human monsters that roam the desert are still called "children of the Fallout."

Brother Francis, weak from fasting in the desert heat, would prefer to return to the abbey for advice, but curiosity impels him to descend the stone steps. At the bottom of the crumbling stairway, he sees a door with this sign:

FALLOUT SURVIVAL SHELTER
Maximum occupancy: 15

> . . . The novice stared at the sign in dismay. Its meaning was plain enough. He had unwittingly broken into the abode (deserted, he prayed) of not just one, but fifteen of the dreadful beings! He groped for his phial of holy water.[17]

Not understanding why the ancients should have built such "marvellous contraptions" to insure the survival of the fearsome Fallouts, Brother Francis begins to regret that Pre-Deluge English was such a complicated and ambiguous language. Analytic languages always confuse him. In the inflectional clarity of Latin, he could be sure exactly what the sign meant, but here in one phrase are three nouns. Which word describes which word? A shelter for Fallout survival? A Fallout for shelter survival? Or survival for Fallout shelters? Taking no chances, he decides to investigate rather than wonder all night if he were being stalked by a Fallout. Inside the shelter, he discovers not simply another cache of printed matter, but priceless "relics" written by the hand of Leibowitz himself. Scholars of the Albertian Order of

---

[17]Ibid., p. 14.

Leibowitz eventually transcribe and make some use of RACING FORM and CIRCUIT DESIGN, two printed pamphlets, but they never successfully decipher the handwritten note reading, "Pound pastrami, can kraut, six bagels--bring home for Emma."[18]

Lexicography, as a process, is not presented in A Canticle for Leibowitz, but the results of faulty reasoning are evident. A word gains meaning through the different contexts in which it is used, but unless the available contexts convey an accurate definition, the meaning of the original word is lost forever. From the few references that have survived, a Fallout could well be defined as a legendary monster. Leibowitz's "Pound pastrami" note is phrased in such a way that pastrami, kraut, and bagels could be articles of clothing, tools, or almost anything. If the note had ended "bring home for supper," at least the items could have been identified as food. Obviously, the author intended these episodes for amusement, but applying the same principle of defining words through faulty contexts, in a language that is no longer spoken, it is possible that a modern lexicographer could unwittingly commit the same type of error.

It is assumed that, in real life, lexicographers do not knowingly record misinformation. Not so in fiction. In compiling items for the Newspeak Dictionary, Big Brother's lexicographers record what they intend for the citizens to

---

[18]Ibid., p. 22.

believe. R. A. Lafferty's "What's the Name of That Town?"[19] also includes "doctored dictionaries," but with a different twist. The central character is a computer with a sense of humor and an insatiable curiosity. In its spare time, it programs itself with information gathered from dictionary-encyclopedias, and then poses questions to its human associates:

> Item: Why, in Hungarian dictionary-encyclopedias of a certain period, is there padding between the words Sik and Sikamlos?
>
> Item: Why is the young of a bear now referred to as a pup when once it may have been known as a cube? . . . There is probably an imperfect erasure working.
>
> Item: Why is the awkward word Coronal used for the simple doubling or return of a rope? Why is not a simpler word used?
>
> Item: Why does Petit Larousse take five lines too many to say almost nothing about the ancient Chibcha Indians of Columbia?
>
> Item: Why are . . . Little Willie verses concerned almost entirely with chewing gum?[20]

These and other seemingly irrelevant questions are prompted by the computer's detection of deletions in dictionaries throughout the world, as preceding entries are padded to fill the hole. The machine then catalogs and analyzes the information that should be given, but is not, and it is able to restore the entries:

---

[19] R. A. Lafferty, "What's the Name of That Town?" Science Fiction Oddities, Griff Conklin, ed. (New York: Berkley Publishing Corporation, 1966).

[20] Ibid., taken from pp. 119-122.

> . . . There really was a large city named Chicago. As <u>Sikago</u>, it left a hole in one Hungarian dictionary-encyclopedia; and the Petit Larousse had to flow French froth about the Chibcha Indians into the place where <u>Chicago</u> had stood. . . . Chicago was a great city. The heart of her downtown was known as the <u>Loop</u>, and one of her baseball teams was named the <u>Cubs</u>. For that reason those two words were forced out of use. They might be evocative. . . . Chicago was the chewing gum capital of the world. The leader in this manufacture was a man named--as well as I can reconstruct it--Wiggly . . . tied in with . . . Little Willy verses about chewing gum.[21]

This unusual application of lexicography utilizes information that is <u>not</u> included in order to discover that the once-existing city of Chicago had been destroyed by some unspecified "unnatural disaster." The world's population was hypnotically induced to forget the existence of the city, and lexicographers throughout the world were called upon to "doctor" dictionaries and encyclopedias by deleting every word that, by association, might break the spell of universal amnesia.

Lafferty's short story is not a literary masterpiece, but it is a vehicle that emphasizes the importance of lexical information. History book references alone could have been expunged, but dictionary entries carry a variety of facts, including semantic facts of word-association, that are beyond the field of pure history. A competent lexicographer is more than historian, more than researcher or sociologist or psychologist or specialist in any one area of linguistics; he is all of these and, in addition, an alert observer and recorder of the language.

---

[21]<u>Ibid</u>., p. 126.

CHAPTER VII

HOW TO LEARN MARTIAN

When a fictional hero lands among an alien people, it usually takes only a few pages for him to become fluent in the alien language. But how, a reader might wonder, does he learn the language without a textbook or a dictionary? The answer is that he learns it in the same way that missionaries have learned unwritten and unexamined tongues, and in the same way that modern linguists compiled grammars and dictionaries and pronunciation guides for unwritten (at least, unwritten in English) languages for the Army Intensive Training Courses at the beginning of the Korean War,[1] and in the same way that John Eliot probably learned the language of the Algonquin Indians during colonial days. Modern writers of fiction do not often illustrate their protagonist's first stumbling efforts to communicate, perhaps because they feel the reader would not be interested or because they themselves do not know the procedure, but the element of language-learning does occasionally appear with some emphasis in fiction.

---

[1] Ornstein and Gage, pp. 60-61, states that over fifty languages were analyzed for this program, and the texts prepared by linguists were geared for rapid learning of the languages in oral communication only. Little or no grammar study was involved, but learning was based on structure and pattern drills.

C. S. Lewis's <u>Out of the Silent Planet</u>, written in 1938 as the first book in a trilogy,[2] is a religious allegory that is, on several levels, a book about communication. An Oxford don named Ransom is kidnapped by two former classmates, one of whom is named Devine, and taken to another planet. Once landed, Ransom escapes his captors and, alone, meets and lives with a race of poetry-loving native creatures until he is summoned by the spiritual overlord of the planet. On his journey there, Ransom meets a second race, the intelligentsia of the planet, and, within the confines of the overlord's palace, a third race of artists and historians. It is here that communication is pictorial, as he sees a stone carving of the planetary system and realizes that he is on the planet that his race calls Mars. Earth, his home planet, has been rudely gouged out of the stone carving,[3] and Ransom learns that he has been brought to this planet by his fellow Earthmen as a sacrificial offering to the creatures in exchange for gold. It is discovered, however, that on an earlier visit,

---

[2] C. S. Lewis, <u>Out of the Silent Planet</u> (New York: Macmillan and Company, 1938). The other two books of the trilogy are <u>Perelandra</u> (1944) and <u>That Hideous Strength</u> (1946). Kingsley Amis comments (<u>New Maps of Hell</u>, p. 28) that the last two books become "increasingly alien," but "Lewis's hrossa, seroni, and pfifltriggi are rational beings and sufficiently like us to merit comparison."

[3] <u>Ibid</u>., p. 119. The stone carving itself is an interesting medium of communication; even with no knowledge of the Greek mythology on our planet, the Malacandrian impressions of planets as gods, with gender and special interest, parallel those of our mythology.

Devine had misunderstood the overlord's request for a third Earthman; the overlord had requested a more intelligent and perceptive man to deliver a message of warning to Earth. That "Ransom becomes a ransom" in the intended destruction of the "bent" planet Earth perhaps lacks in subtlety of plot, but this element is one of literary criticism. For linguistic analysis, at least Lewis did not simply say that Ransom "learned the language."

Following his initial encounter with an alien creature, during which he realizes that it has a language, Ransom begins to make mental notes for the "dazzling project" of writing the first grammar of a nonhuman tongue. The creature calls itself a "hross" and Ransom identifies himself as a "man," which the creature pronounces "hman." It touches the earth and says "handra," points to the mountains and says "harandra" and to the valley and says "handramit." With <u>handra</u>, <u>harandra</u>, and <u>handramit</u>, Ransom identifies earth, high-earth, and earth-low, and he notes the ellipsis of the <u>h</u> in <u>har</u>(h)<u>andra</u>. In the village, he builds his vocabulary and his grammatical knowledge: a male creature is a <u>hross</u>, two are <u>hrossa</u>; a female is a <u>hress</u>, and two are <u>hressni</u>; remembering that Devine had spoken of a creature called a <u>sorn</u>, he learns that its plural is <u>séroni</u> and that the Séroni live in the <u>harandra</u>, or "high-earth," the mountains. Having become accustomed to the initial <u>h</u> of most words, including personal names like Hnohra, Hyoi, Hrikki, and Hrinha, Ransom is surprised when he later meets the race of Séroni and hears them say "man" instead of "hman." The speech of the hrossa is, in fact, a dialect, and the other two races call them rossa and pronounce most of their common words without the initial h. "Hman" and "man" are simply dialect variants of the same language.

Lewis demonstrates, rather than explains, how Ransom learns this Martian language, and the alien words are always used in a definitive context at first. Having established that this planet is called Malacandra (Malac-handra), and remembering an incident in which a talkative little hross is told "Thulc!" by his reprimanding father, Ransom is prepared to understand when he is told that his home planet is called Thulcandra, the "quiet earth" or "silent earth," because all communication with it has been severed. All of this Lewis does without translations, and at the end of the story, a reader registers words like handra, thulc, hnakra (a shark-like creature), hnéraki (hnakra-hunters), and hnau (mortals, men, not gods) as easily as if he could actually speak the Malacandrian language.

The reader does, in fact, read Malacandrian. He must, in order to know all the objects and peoples that have their existence only in this imaginary world. An eldil is the semi-visible spirit of an "unbodied" hnau--not "dead" as in our world--and eldila are among the characters in the story. Ransom learns the difference between wondelone "to long for" and hluntheline "to yearn for"; a hnau might wondelon for an audience with the <u>oyarsa</u> (divine ruler) of his world, but he <u>hlunthelin</u> for a <u>hnakra</u> steak for dinner. Through the progress of this novel, such words not only become familiar to the reader, but they assume connotations and complexity that would be difficult to define simply.

Lewis supplies his protagonist with a native speaker who, although not bilingual, is cooperative. Modern descriptive linguists who are involved in the same type of language analysis must also use whatever materials are available,[4] but the present state of descriptive grammar owes a great debt to the men whose efforts and experiments laid its foundation. It is doubtful that any writer of fiction could invent an imaginary language whose grammatical counterparts are not present in at least one of the world languages now analyzed and recorded. Even when, like Lewis, an author writes words in an actual imaginary language, he can usually supply enough nouns, verbs, and adjectives to allow any reader who remembers his high school English to give a rudimentary description of the grammar of the language. There is a catch, of course, because the nontechnical reader is certain to think of languages in terms of English grammar; any word not falling neatly into one of the eight traditional parts of speech will

---

[4]Robert Lowie, The History of Ethnological Theory (New York: Holt, Rinehart and Winston, 1937), p. 136-37. Other materials can be written in the native language, but not yet translated into English; a literate native can supply translations, or a linguist's knowledge of native folklore can provide key words with which to begin.

be lost to him. One alert to the principles involved in descriptive linguistics, on the other hand, might be more receptive to the idea that "the English way" is not the only way a language can be organized.

The descriptive branch of linguistics was, at one time, unrelated to the field of English. The recognized pioneer of field work in the area is the German-born Franz Boas, who, in 1899, became the first professor of anthropology at Columbia University.[5] Boas, most interested in the cultural branch of anthropology, schooled his students in objective observation and description, as they studied the cultural traits of American Indian tribes, and Boas considered language an important ethnological factor. Just as he emphasized "cultural relativism"--the rejection of absolutes or value judgments, regarding cultural traditions only in terms of that culture--he trained his students to approach indigenous Indian languages, most of them unwritten and hitherto unexamined, with the same open-minded objectivity. The purpose behind "linguistic relativism" was not to judge a language as "simple" or "primitive" or even "complicated,"[6] but to record it as

---

[5]Gleason, p. 40.

[6]Felix M. Keesing, Cultural Anthropology: The Science of Custom (New York: Holt, Rinehart and Winston, 1962), pp. 178-79 and 375. Keesing suggests that one of the most "ethnologically revealing documents" is the mail-order catalog!

accurately as possible, analyze its grammatical structure, and describe the language for itself without trying to force its grammatical structure into any known pattern.

Accomplishing this objective was not easy. Under ideal circumstances, the student could locate a native speaker who had become literate or bilingual. Then the native informant could be asked to translate certain carefully structured sentences into his native tongue in order to provide a basic working knowledge of the Indian language. Lacking a bilingual informant, as happened in a majority of the cases, Boas and his students developed a linguistic procedure by which the unwritten language could be broken down into increasingly smaller elements, each step carefully recorded, and eventually described in terms of grammatical structure and phonology.[7]

Boas was a great anthropologist and teacher, but he never wrote a text propounding his ideas. Our knowledge of his work in the field comes from a later reconstruction of his lectures through the class notes of some of his students--A. L. Kroeber, Margaret Mead, Robert Lowie, Edward Sapir, and others--published in 1911 as a book entitled Handbook of American Indian Languages, for which Boas wrote a lengthy introduction.[8] Each

---

[7]Melville J. Herskovits, Cultural Anthropology (New York: Alfred A. Knopf, Inc., 1955), p. 4.

[8]Lowie, p. 129. This book is dated in relation to its technological information, but it is of great value because Lowie took his degree under Boas and he provides personal observations and insight into Boas's theories.

student concentrated his attention upon that aspect of culture in which he was most interested. Edward Sapir, whose interest was language, became a linguistic anthropologist; as a teacher himself, he later taught Benjamin Lee Whorf, who thought of himself as more firmly based in language and, therefore, as an anthropological linguist.[9] Boas taught Sapir, who taught Whorf, and through the work of these three men, the role of language description and analysis was shifted from a purely anthropological concern to one of linguistic importance.

In recording the Indian languages, Boas and his students soon realized the inadequacies of the existing system of phonetic transcription, and they supplemented it with a further breakdown into phonemic subdivisions, now called "allophones." Edward Sapir, the first American anthropologist to recognize the significance of sound variations undetectable in writing, is now recognized as the first descriptive linguist to base his theory on the phoneme,[10] although later linguists have supplied most of the terminology. Allophones are those varied pronunciations of a single written letter, t for example, as they are conditioned by surrounding sounds: "tart" contains two different pronunciations of t, the first beginning with a puff of air and the second ending with a complete stoppage of air with the tongue. "Suprasegmental phonemes" are those vocal factors of stress, pitch, and

---

[9]Ibid., pp. 136-37.

[10]Gleason, p. 43.

juncture that distinguish between "the blackbird" and "the black bird," between "I scream" and "ice cream," and between "It is John" and "It is John?" The unconscious use of such allophones and suprasegmental phonemes is natural to a native speaker of any language, but it is these factors of oral and aural importance that often result in the "foreign accent" of a non-native speaker who might write the language perfectly. And it was the necessity of recording these variations in pronunciation that led Edward Sapir to add phonemic description to phonetic transcription, enabling other phoneticists to record unusual phonemes such as the "grunts and clicks" of the Hottentots, the implosives in other African languages, the "whistle speech" of the natives of Gomera, and the "musical" grammar of tonal languages.

Such painstaking, handwritten phonetic transcriptions have now been simplified by today's "hardware-oriented linguists" with their tape recorders and sound spectrographs and computerized materials,[11] but the methodology is basically unchanged when dealing with an unwritten language.[12] When linguists can find a bilingual informant, he can be asked to translate certain structured sentences, which are then recorded for later

---

[11] Ornstein and Gage, p. 60.

[12] Since its foundation in 1943, S. I. Hayakawa has been editor of *ETC: A Review of General Semantics*, a quarterly journal devoted to the descriptive study of language. Many of the articles have been written by foreign students, themselves bilingual, on linguistic factors appearing in unwritten dialects of little known languages unfamiliar even to linguists. The journal contains much esoteric information.

analysis. The material actually used by Boas and his students has been unavailable,[13] but the following are examples of such structured sentences:

>This is a man.
>This is a woman.
>This is a child.
>This is a house.
>This is a dog.

By eliminating the repetitious sounds, the words for man, woman, child, house, and dog can be isolated as vocabulary. Then:

>These are men.
>These are women.
>These are children.
>These are houses.
>These are dogs.

Using more than these five examples, a comparison of the isolated words can establish a pattern for forming plurals, and other structure patterns can be provided in order to discover other grammatical elements, such as gender, word order, placement of modifiers, and inflections. It is imperative, however, that linguists do not actively look for "inflections" or "modifiers" or any other known grammatical form, but after establishing the function or position of a class of words, they may find that traditional terminology is the most accurate

---

[13]An excellent and entertaining exercise in analyzing Swahili sentences is found in the workbook accompanying H. A. Gleason's *An Introduction to Descriptive Linguistics* (New York: Henry Holt and Co., 1956).

means of description.

Lacking a bilingual native informant, other methods can be used. The "immediate constituent" system, more sophisticated and developed since Boas's day, is still effective.[14] As the informant speaks in his native tongue, his uninterrupted speech--no matter how long--is recorded as an "utterance." The utterance is broken down into single sentences, usually identifiable by longer pauses; the sentences are broken into phrases within the sentence, the phrases into words, the words into morphemes (and identified as either "bound" or "free" morphemes), the phoneme into allphones) and each step carefully recorded. Phonetic analysis can record the total number of sounds present in the language, and an analysis of all the recorded material can provide a description of the grammatical structure of the language. The most thorough and most recent article dealing with the transcription of unwritten languages is Charles F. Hockett's "How to Learn Martian," which must be read in its entirety to be appreciated; it will be discussed more fully later, as a blending of scientific facts and science fiction.

When a writer of fiction gives a lengthy utterance in an imaginary language and then supplies an English translation,

---

[14]Harry Hoijer, "Language and Writing," Man, Culture and Society, Harry L. Shapiro, ed. (New York: Oxford University Press, 1956), pp. 203-206. See also Eugene Nida's Learning a Foreign Language: Handbook for Missionaries (New York: National Council of Churches of Christ in the U.S.A., 1950).

he becomes vulnerable to analysis, although, admittedly, the average reader may have neither the skill nor the inclination to do so. Mention has already been made of J. R. R. Tolkien's The Lord of the Ring trilogy, with its appendixes at the end of the third volume. Appendix F, under the description of the Ent language, includes this statement:

> The strange words and names that the Hobbits record as used . . . by Ents are thus Elvish, or fragments of Elf-speech strung together in Ent-fashion. Some are Quenya: as Taurelilómëa-tumbalemorna Tumbaletaurëa Lómëanor, which may be rendered "forestmanyshadowed-deepvalleyblack Deepvalleyforested Gloomyland," and by which . . . is meant, more or less: "there is a black shadow in the deep dales of the forest."[15]

Tolkien is vulnerable. Here is an utterance in an imaginary language, with a word-for-word transcription and an English translation. This utterance was selected because of its length and the available translation, and assuming the omniscience of the author to substitute for a native speaker, it can be evaluated by its immediate constituents.

Recording the words as an utterance is the first step, and the translation identifies it as a single sentence, which would be the next step. It is a four-word sentence:

```
        (1)              (2)           (3)         (4)
   Taurelilómëa-tumbalemorna     Tumbaletaurëa   Lómëanor
```

---

[15]Tolkien, The Return of the King, p. 510.

Further analysis may proceed in this manner.

Words (2) and (3) repeat a phrase:

<u>tumbalemorna</u>   <u>Tumbaletaurëa</u>
deep-valley-black   deep-valley-forested

Therefore, <u>morna</u> means "black" and <u>taurëa</u> means "forested." A form of <u>taurëa</u> "forested" also appears in Word (1) as <u>Taure</u> "forest," and the morpheme <u>-ëa</u> is repeated in Word (4) in <u>Lómëa</u> "shadowed, gloomy." <u>Tumbale</u> means "deep-valley," but it is uncertain whether the portion of the phrase meaning "valley" is <u>bale</u> or simply <u>le</u>.

So far, by ignoring <u>nor</u> in Word (4), it is possible to make these observations:

1. The Ent language is inflectional, with holophrastic, or polysynthetic, compounding of words.
2. Nouns usually end in <u>-e</u> (<u>taure</u>, *<u>lóme</u>, <u>bale</u> or <u>le</u>).[16]
3. Adjectives-from-nouns are formed by suffixing the bound morpheme <u>-ëa</u> (<u>taurëa</u>, <u>lómëa</u>, *<u>balëa</u> or *<u>lëa</u>).
4. The Ent language is presumably verbless.

Then, eliminating the nouns and adjectives-from-nouns, the remaining words are <u>li</u> "many," <u>morna</u> "black," and <u>tumbale</u>, of which either <u>tumba</u> or <u>tum</u> means "deep." Traditional grammar would classify all three words as adjectives, but descriptive grammar recognizes that all adjectives do not perform the same function. "Determiners" are words such as <u>the</u>, <u>one</u>, <u>some</u>,

---

[16]Following the procedure used in historical linguistics, * indicates a hypothetically constructed word.

several, and these, whose function is to identify or limit, and "qualifiers" are words such as large, round, empty, and friendly, which describe. Li "many" is a determiner, morna "black" is a qualifier ending in a, and by analogy it can be assumed that tumba, also ending in a, is the other qualifier. Since the compound tumbale means "deep-valley," identifying tumba as "deep" indicates that le, not bale, is the correct word for "valley."

Two more observations may now be added:

5. Qualifiers end in a (although two examples are not sufficient evidence).

6. Determiners end in i (with even less evidence).

Syntactically, only a conjecture can be made. The "head word," or main noun, comes first in the first word, medially in the two middle words, and last in the last word, as it moves progressively toward the end of each compound word.[17] However, even on such scanty evidence as if offered in this four-word sentence, assuming the morphological analysis to be valid, a descriptive linguist could reverse the process and begin to construct words in the Ent language:

*lilëataure "many-valleyed-forest"

*litaurëale "many-forested-valley

---

[17] Nor, as the only noun which does not end in -e, is also the only noun appearing in terminal position. Certainly, the other open-ended nouns help the flow of the sentence, but it is possible that -e is a morpheme that would be dropped from any noun in terminal position; nor would, in that case, appear as *nore if it were used in initial or medial position.

*morntaurëanor "black-forested-land"

*mornalómëanor "black-shadowed-land"

*mornalëanor "black-valleyed-land"

According to linguistic criteria, Ent is a speakable language. If Ents existed and a person should want to learn their language, he could begin with this description and have a vocabulary of nine words; he would know how to form adjectives from a noun, and with the morpheme -ëa as a structure signal, he could identify other adjectives in this class (as they appear in the conversation with native Ents) and add to his vocabulary of nouns. Tolkien himself supplies other information that would ordinarily be derived from language analysis. Ent is an unwritten language, but Appendix E "Writing and Spelling" contains a phonetic table, complete with dialect variants among the different language groups, that becomes a pronunciation guide to the Ent language. Alphabets in ancient scripts are given for other languages, but (as Tolkien explains) the Ent language, as well as others, he has transcribed into English symbols that will be familiar to the reader. Appendix F also contains ethnological and cultural-linguistic information about the Ents:

> The language that they had made was unlike all others: slow, sonorous, agglomerated, repetitive, indeed long-winded; formed of a multiplicity of vowel-shades and distinctions of tone and quantity which even the loremasters of the Eldar had not attempted to represent in

writing. They used it only among themselves; but they had no need to keep it secret, for no others could learn it.[18]

"Vowel-shades" and "distinctions of tone and quantity" are simply other terms for "suprasegmental phonemes" of stress, pitch, and juncture; these phonemic variations are discussed in connection with the phonetic table in Appendix E[19] with almost unbelievable thoroughness.

But no one will ever learn the Ent language or converse with an Ent. Even descriptive linguists do not necessarily analyze an unwritten language, or an already written language, for the purpose of learning to speak it themselves; their analysis can be used as a grammatical guide, but its purpose is to describe the language, and this language only, for its own sake. Languages do have a systematic arrangement of parts, and the more variety of arrangements that a linguist has recognized and analyzed, the more knowledge he can apply to the decipherment of other languages.

If a linguist should take the time to analyze a single sentence from an imaginary language, placed in an obscure corner of an appendix attached to a book clearly labeled as

---

[18] Tolkien, The Return of the King, p. 510.

[19] Critic Neil Isaacs wonders about the juncture that should be involved in pronouncing the name of the naive and gullible character Halfast. Is it "Hal-fast" or "Half-ast"? Neil D. Isaacs, "On the Possibilities of Writing Tolkien Criticism," Tolkien and the Critics, p. 11.

a "fairy tale," and, surprisingly, he should discover that the author has carefully and skillfully made the sentence as linguistically authentic as possible, then it seems that the result should have some value. As a tool in literary criticism, it should help to evaluate the merit of both the book and the author. In descriptive linguistics, it is another unique grammatical system whose analysis adds to the present store of knowledge about language and languages. As an ethnological factor, even though fictitious, it helps to analyze the cultural traits of the fictitious society. Linguistic anthropology and anthropological linguistics--depending upon which discipline has the emphasis--may both profit. Language description must necessarily be an interdisciplinary science; anthropologists study the culture that speaks a language, and linguists study the language spoken by a culture.

CHAPTER VIII

WHAT PEOPLE MEAN AND HOW CARROTS SAY IT

"I didn't kill nobody" is not a confession of guilt. It would probably never occur to a jury to question the grammatical logic involved, because the meaning is clear enough. Beautiful girls are "slender," but homely ones are "skinny"; a friend is "stocky," an enemy is "fat." A person is called tenacious, persistent, adamant, or pig-headed, depending on the attitude of the speaker or the impression he means to create. "A portly matron" is not the same as "a fat woman," although the two may be identical in size.

That semantics plays an important role in ordinary speech is a fact of life, and anyone who is deliberately tactful or abusive in his choice of words is using semantics, whether he is consciously aware of it or not. The term "semantics" is not an unusual one in everyday speech, and the average person probably understands that semantics involves using a word or expression whose connotation conveys a meaning or suggestion beyond its factual information. However, if he knows only that much, and if he assumes that the science of semantics is concerned only with word-selection, and if he thinks that it is only he who plays semantic games with other people, and if he thinks that semantics is strictly an academic subject, then he has no more than touched one small part of its range of study.

Semantics, or semasiology, is defined as "the scientific study of the relations between signs, or symbols, and what they mean, or denote, and of behavior in its psychological and sociological aspects as it is influenced by signs,"[1] meaning, in short, studying the ways in which people communicate their experiences. The science of semantics is usually considered a branch of linguistics, which it is when communication is verbal, but it also involves the psychological effects of communication, the sociological implications, the cultural and environmental habits of communication, and various other specific areas, each of which demands alliance with another discipline. The science of semantics is concerned, basically, with the process of communication in its broadest sense, but modern semanticists are interested foremost in identifying those points at which human understanding may break down or go astray or become distorted--those points most likely to produce a "communication gap." Somewhere along the route that an idea must travel, from one human mind to another, are certain hazardous spots, and these spots are the semanticist's laboratory.

The laboratory of semantics is also the playground of fiction. Utopian people communicate with "perfect understanding," a concept which is usually as dull in fiction as

---

[1]"Semantics," Webster's New World Dictionary of the English Language, College Edition (New York: The World Publishing Co., 1964), p. 1324.

it would be in real life, but skillful manipulators of those themes possible only in science fiction-fantasy--space and time travel--can create communication gaps that modern semanticists never dreamed of. Semantics is the study of <u>human</u> communication, and all of its subjects of study, no matter what nationality, have common biological functions and physiological forms and verbal languages. A writer of fantasy can alter all of that, and he can create communication problems that have no modern parallel or precedent.

To consider the function of semantics, or semasiology, a lexicon definition of the science is inadequate. Polish-born Alfred Korzybski is called the "father of semantics," and S. I. Hayakawa is usually acknowledged as the nation's specialist in "general semantics," but the nebulous differences between "semantics" and "semasiology," and between "semantics" and "general semantics," are not explained by a definition. As one critic has observed, a science is often definable according to whether it is an "ology" or an "ics." A venerable, academic "ology" is the study of something specific, as ichthyology is the study of fish, and it suggests academic isolation and scholarly research. An energetic and somewhat mysterious "ics," on the other hand, as "cybernetics," suggests a method of attack on life's problems; it can be defined only in terms of what its specialists do, and any description would probably begin with "It's all a matter of . . . ."[2]

---

[2] Anatol Rapoport, "What Is Semantics?" <u>The Use and Misuse of Language</u>, pp. 11 and 14.

Alfred Korzybski was a semasiologist, and modern Korzybski-ites still speak in terms of "nonverbal levels," "extensional levels," and "colloidal levels." S. I. Hayakawa is a semanticist who is also a teacher and university president, writer of textbooks and articles, editor of a scholarly journal on semantics, and, in addition, an astute commentator on the application of semantics in modern society. Hayakawa speaks in terms of "maps," "territories," and "cows."

The communication of information from one person to another, says Hayakawa,[3] is like making a map of a territory. Just as a plot of land, a territory, does not necessarily have the trees and rivers that a nature-loving cartographer might pencil into his map, neither does a person necessarily have the attributes or defects that a biased observer might suggest into his "map" of description. A mother's "little angel" might be a teacher's "little brat," two different "maps" of the same six-year-old boy. Maps can be misleading, and the only means of verifying the accuracy of the map is to visit the territory. The only obstacle to this type of verification is that, more often than not, the "territory" no longer exists. An event in history, a transient mood of one person, a remembered conversation, a traffic accident--all of these territories are no longer accessible, and we are dependent on the

---

[3]See the chapter entitled "The Map Is Not the Territory" in Hayakawa's Language in Thought and Action (New York: Harcourt, Brace and Company, 1949), especially p. 17.

maps spoken or written by others. The "map-and-territory" analogy is not intended to discredit the integrity of the observer, however; deliberate falsehoods aside, the observer might have the incident perfectly pictured in his mind, but his method of describing it, perhaps in choice of words or use of gestures, leads the listener to recreate a distorted view of the "territory" in his own mind. The listener hears what is <u>said</u>, not what is <u>meant</u>; hence, a "communication gap."[4]

According to Hayakawa, the only possible means of communicating an exact, complete, and unbiased item of information is to point to its referent. This is mind-to-mind, telepathic communication, eliminating all the potential pitfalls in word, facial expression, gesture, or other signals, that might reshape an idea in transit. For obvious reasons, real people do not communicate by telepathy, but many people would no doubt consider this silent communication a boon in our cacophonous world. As Anthony Burgess says, "I have to look forward to the possibility of a world without words, a wordless, intuitive world, like a technological extension of the action of consciousness."[5] Telepathic communication does

---

[4]This article appeared in The Houston Chronicle (February 7, 1971), p. 1:
    Denver (UPI) U.S. District Judge William Doyle says he thinks it was just a mixup in words. A businessman told the judge that the cause of justice is not served "when you get promiscuous on the bench."
    "I knew he meant permissive," the judge said later.

[5]Anthony Burgess. "The Electric Grape," The American Scholar (Autumn, 1966), 720.

occur often in science fiction-fantasy, always as the language of an alien society or a super-species. Telepathy is not a new idea in literature, but now more freely used, it indicates "a rapid and penetrating communication by short-cutting the more conventional medium of language . . . and it has paralleled the emergence of disciplines specifically dealing with communications, such as significs, semantics, and cybernetics."[6] In fiction, the presence of a telepathic language has only one purpose: to emphasize the importance of semantics in spoken language.

Such telepathic communication is a feature in Isaac Asimov's "What Is This Thing Called Love?"[7] In the alien species, signals are transmitted via "color patches," located somewhere on the face, and through the changing hues, pure concepts are transferred from one person to another. On an intergalactic spy mission, the alien Botax has been secreted on Earth in order to gather cultural data on earthmen, but the only material he has had access to (besides overhearing conversations) is a periodical with the two-concept title play and boy, which he renders orally as "Recreationlad." Botax has learned to imitate "native sounds" and simulate

---

[6] Robert Plank, "Communication in Science Fiction," The Use and Misuse of Language, p. 147.

[7] Isaac Asimov, "What Is This Thing Called Love?" Science Fiction Oddities, Groff Conklin, ed. (New York: Berkley Publishing Corporation, 1966), pp. 16-28.

earthly language, but he still thinks in pure concepts--<u>play</u>, <u>diversion</u>, <u>recreation</u>, <u>sport</u>, <u>fun</u> are, to him, one and the same. When his superior officer arrives on this planet for a progress report, the spy is able to flash to him the results of his study: one, the terran species is composed of two forms, the exact difference between them uncertain, except that "one bulges where the other does not"; two, the species, according to the reference materials consulted, is inordinately preoccupied with the reproductive process; three, this process concerns inter-form cooperation of some sort and, therefore, must be indicative of a conspiracy.

Having come from a unisexual world where one simply sprouts a bud when he feels the urge, the two aliens agree that earthmen must be a potentially dangerous species. The Captain, however, dissatisfied with the gaps in his underling's knowledge, orders that one specimen of each form be produced for an experiment.

Telepathic concept-transference, nonverbal and entirely denotative in nature, conveys only accurate "meanings." There is no provision for connotative suggestions, cultural or personal idea-association, or figurative imagery, as the aliens discover when they kidnap a Bronx housewife and a tired laborer, complete strangers, and politely request them to "cooperate."

"Hey, it talks!" said Charlie. "What do you mean, cooperate?"

"Both of you. With each other," said Botax.
"Oh?" Charlie looked at Marge. "You know what he means, lady?"
"Ain't got no idea whatsoever," she answered loftily.[8]

Botax the spy, however, has gleaned enough native terminology from "Recreationlad" to outline to the Captain his understanding of the steps in the ritual. First, the larger form must comment on the "ivory skin" of the smaller form. "Ivory," he flashes importantly to the Captain, "is the tusky material of one of the large sub-intelligent creatures on the planet," although he himself is not sure what part tusks play in the ritual. Then the two forms must "kiss."

"And what is that?"
"There is no flash for it, Captain. I just made it up for the occasion. Essentially, it consists of placing the speaking-and-eating apparatus of one against the equivalent apparatus of the other . . . "
"Will nausea never cease?" groaned the Captain.
". . . they clasp each other with limbs and indulge madly in burning kisses, to translate as nearly as possible . . . . Here, look at this example, 'He held the girl, his mouth avid on her lips.'"
"Maybe one creature was devouring the other," said the Captain.
"Not at all," said Botax impatiently. "Those were burning kisses."
"How do you mean, burning? Combustion takes place?"[9]

Remembering that this native language has many words (for some unknown reason) to refer to a single concept, Botax improvises and substitutes another synonym that he has overheard.

---

[8]Ibid., p. 20.

[9]Ibid., p. 25.

This time, the earthlings have no doubt what he means by "cooperate," but their reaction is a terrible, inexplicable furor. And they flatly refuse to cooperate.

The culmination of this ritual, as far as Botax has learned, ends immediately after the "kiss," and the result is a "love," which is presumably another synonym for the young of the species. Marge agrees to kiss Charlie, only to avoid contact with Botax (". . . this dress cost $24.95 . . . . Just don't touch it with slime, for God's sake!") and the Captain, mollified, sits down to wait.

> But the moments passed and the Captain's flashes turned slowly to a brooding orange, while Botax's nearly dimmed out altogether.
> Botax finally asked hesitantly, "Pardon me, madam, but when will you bud?"
> "When will I _what_?"
> "Bear young?"
> "I've got a kid."
> "I mean bear young _now_."
> "I should say not. I ain't ready for another kid yet."
> "What? What?" demanded the Captain. "What's she saying?"
> "It seems," said Botax, weakly, "that she does not intend to have young at the moment."[10]

The story ends as Botax, crushed and probably demoted, returns to his unisexual planet as he endures the Captain's tirade. "You've upset me, turned my stomach, nauseated me, disgusted me with the whole notion . . . . After thinking of the foul habits you have been describing, I don't think I'll

---

[10] _Ibid._, pp. 26-27.

ever bud again!" These aliens understand neither the need for synonyms in the early language nor the attitude of the earthmen toward what is obviously only a biological function; as a result, they do not understand earthmen or their culture.

There are two semantic truths illustrated here. One is that concepts--pure, platonic ideals--allow no provision for emotion or sentiment, no imagination, no variety of expression. Everything is taken at its literal value. Concepts have no aesthetic significance, and species that communicate telepathically are a literal-minded, humorless, unromantic people. The second truth, interrelated with the first, is that the semantic symbols of a language are expressions of the cultural values of its speakers, forming the criteria by which they often judge other peoples. Writers of fiction who use telepathic communication in their stories rarely ignore the opportunity to point out the cultural relativity involved. Science fiction, which allows an alien view of the whole human race, often lends a new perspective to man's view of himself. The "foul habits," such as kissing, are ones that we earthmen accept without question because we view them from within, but aliens have a different perspective:

> "And those? What purpose do they have?"
> "I think," said Botax with considerable hesitation, "that they are used to feed the young."
> "The young eat them?" asked the Captain with every evidence of deep distress.

"Not exactly. The objects produce a fluid which the young consume."
"Consume a fluid from a living body? Yech-h-h."[11]

Marge calls the aliens "slimy bug-eyed monsters," and the Captain calls earthmen "nauseating two-form creatures." Each judges the other, not in relation to the culture he represents, but in terms of his own experiences. The humor involved is outside of the story, between author and reader, as the reader is forced to see something of himself in both aliens and earthmen. Virtually every fictional occurrence of telepathic communication illustrates the advantages and superiority of spoken language.

Telepathy itself is not fantasy, and scientists of the twentieth century have become increasingly interested in psychic phemonema, clairvoyance, and ESP as a utilitarian means of communication. Astronaut Edgar Mitchell, long interested in ESP, requested permission from NASA that he be allowed to conduct some unofficial experiments in psychic communication during the Apollo 14 moon flight during the first part of February, 1971.[12] Parapsychologists at Duke University developed a set of cards to be used, and they selected Olof Jonson, known in parapsychological circles for his work in ESP and telepathy, as Mitchell's contact on Earth. During the nine-day expedition,

---

[11]Ibid., p. 23.

[12]Colin Leinster, "Experiments in Geology -- and Telepathy," Life, LXX (February 26, 1971), 28-29.

man's second landing on the moon, Mitchell conducted six experiments of six minutes each, sending a total of 150 messages to Jonson, who then recorded his impressions and turned the results over to the scientists at Duke University. As of this writing, results of this experiment have not been released, and even Jonson does not know how accurately he received the telepathic messages sent by astronaut Mitchell from outer space. Jonson claims, however, that at times the message was strong and that he feels confident about the potential of telepathic communication.

Meanwhile on earth, modern man communicates in other ways--words, gestures, grimaces or smiles or raised eyebrows--and he reacts to stimuli such as colors and sounds. Semasiologists record gestures and what they "mean," and they measure reactions to stimuli in relation to cultural and environmental conditioning; as for semanticists and what they do--it's all a matter of who they are.

A semanticist usually applies his knowledge to another profession, one which can benefit by knowing exactly the ways in which "saying" and "meaning" can differ. Factual, unslanted reporting is an art requiring a careful selection of words with no strong overtones of personal opinion; slanted, "yellow journalism" is an art that utilizes the same skills. Public relations and consumer advertizing are even more fertile fields for a knowledge of semantics, as advertizing methods are based on idea-associations. Consumers are more likely to select a bottle labeled "Loving Care" than one labeled "Hair Rinse"; janitors perform more efficiently if they are called "building engineers"; readers will always read the words printed in a contrasting color; elderly people gain dignity in being called "senior citizens"; and any product, whether furnace or lawn mower, rises in sales when it hints at higher social status or marital bliss, in addition to keeping feet warm or cutting grass.[13] Idea-associations, not simply words, are the basis of consumer research, and the task of the semanticist is to find exactly the right symbol to stimulate the acquisitive nature of the averagely affluent, pleasure-seeking, status-conscious, romantic, ego-centered, typical American consumer. These symbols--colors, shapes and forms, the stance and gestures in a picture, the "catchy tune"--all are manipulated with an adeptness that would dismay the average consumer, whose psyche is the intended target.

The professions just mentioned represent the use of semantic knowledge that comes from an inside view of one's own cultural symbols of meaning. Ordinary tourists often recognize that the same signals that have meaning to them might have no meaning, or have an entirely different meaning, to speakers of a different language. Intercultural semantics presents a

---

[13] An excellent analysis of advertizing methods appears in "The Art of Advertizing," Better Language and Thinking, Rachel Salisbury, ed. (New York: Appleton-Century Crofts, Inc., 1955), pp. 109-116. Hayakawa explains "Why the Edsel Laid an Egg: Motivational Research vs. the Reality Principle" in his The Use and Misuse of Language, pp. 169-174.

different kind of problem and a more complex solution.

International translators, news analysts, or interpreters must know not only two or more languages, but the cultural symbols of communication that accompany the cultural conditioning of the speakers. A professional of this type must know the "meaning" suggested in one language which would be unintentionally transmitted by a literal translation. He must then translate meaning or attitude instead of merely words, and he must be able to interpret gestures and sounds, as well. The "tsk tsk" of an American ("Shame!") and of a Spaniard (frustration) and of a speaker of Arabic ("No!") must be properly recognized according to the languages of both the speaker and the spoken-to. A simple _no_ is understood by a speaker of Arabic, whose culture includes bargaining, to be an invitation for further negotiation, while a _no_ of sufficient definiteness to an Arab would be one of discourteous proportions in English. In French culture, a camel is the most repulsive of beasts, but a Frenchman's ". . . like a camel," to convey the same meaning to an Arab, would have to be translated ". . . like a dog."[14] Knowing the proper title

---

[14] Edmund S. Glenn, "Semantic Difficulties in International Communication," The Use and Misuse of Language, p. 49-50. Glenn also illustrates, with cartoons, how speakers of different languages do communicate with perfect clarity; one, captioned "The Language of East-West Diplomacy" shows a European thumbing his nose at an American, who is answering with an equally rude gesture; a line of bandaged, little creatures hobbling along with crutches is captioned "Words--Returning from an International Conference."

of address is important and, when foreign dignitaries mingle on a social basis, it is advantageous to know how much attention should be paid to the wife (or wives) of each man, whether to sit in his presence, whether to offer him alcoholic beverage, which gestures or expressions might give offense. This knowledge, in diplomatic circles, is called protocol, and it is so important to international relations that the President's cabinet includes a Chief of Protocol. It is the responsibility of this "chief semanticist" to advise the President and all personnel concerned, in advance of an international affair of state, of its potential problems in communication.

These are only a few of the "things that semanticists do," but their common denominator is one of human communication, the ways that people express their ideas, and the ways that those expressions can be misinterpreted. Assuming that there is a limit to the number of emotions capable in human experience, and that there is a limit to the number of facial and physiological and manual gestures capable of the human body, and there is a limit to the number of sounds that can be produced by vocal organs, then it is also logical to assume that any cultural group, in expressing its own experiences, will inadvertently duplicate the identical signal chosen by another cultural group to express something entirely different. And they will use a different set of gestures and sounds to express identical ideas. This theory, in essence, is the basic cause of human misunderstanding and lack of accurate human communication. Human beings may not agree on ideology, but they are more likely to do so if they can at least understand the ideas in question.

It is no coincidence that <u>communicate</u> and <u>commune</u> derived from the same source. Each carries the connotation of the other, a theme which pervades Robert Heinlein's <u>Stranger in a Strange Land</u>,[15] "a provocative novel of quasi-pantheistic religion . . . coupled with some intriguing variations of the . . . theory of linguistic relativity."[16] Valentine Michael Smith, the protagonist, was born during the first expedition to Mars and raised by the Martians after the death of the other members of the expedition. Now, twenty-five years later, he has been returned to Earth by crewmen of the second expedition, man by ancestry but Martian by environment and thought. What is important is that Michael thinks and reacts according to his Martian cultural standards, and simple acts and gestures have different meaning to him. On the desert planet of Mars, water means life; the sharing of water, or drinking together, becomes a religious sacrament and an act of unity and brotherhood. When Michael wakes in the hospital, the nurse who offers him a glass of water is unprepared for his reaction to such a routine act. But it is a ritualistic act

---

[15] Robert Heinlein, <u>Stranger in a Strange Land</u> (New York: Berkley Publishing Corporation, 1961).

[16] Willis E. McNelly, "Linguistic Relativity in Middle High Martian," <u>The CEA Critic</u>, XXX (March, 1968), 4.

to Michael meaning a unity so elevated that mistrust is impossible, an oath of eternal friendship, a marriage vow, a common declaration of faith in God, an act of communion.

All of these concepts are expressed in the word <u>grok</u>, the only Martian word used in the book, and one requiring the entire book to define. Through the sequence of actions by Michael and his friends, the Martian concept of "grok" gains extensional meanings in our culture and abstracts the earthly concepts common in love, friendship, allegiance, communion, worship, understanding, unity of spirit, and human communication. This concept, having no single symbol in English, finds perfect expression in the Martian "grok," which gains in significance throughout the book. There is humor, especially with the first encounters between Michael and this alien environment, but the humor lies generally, again, between author and reader, and the message of the entire book is one of communication and communion.

Michael and his circle of friends form a type of cult, the ritualistic act of sharing water symbolic of their common unity, and through their association and Michael's behavioral examples, "grok" expresses a way of life and, in the words of one of the characters,

> . . . even antithetical concepts. It means "fear," it means "love," it means "hate,"--for by the Martian 'map' you cannot hate anything unless you grok it, understand it so thoroughly that you merge with it and it merges with you--then you can hate. . . . Grok means to understand so

thoroughly that the observer becomes a part of the observed--to blend, merge, intermarry, lose identity in group experience.[17]

In its earthly context, "grok" also takes on a number of extensional modifications culturally and emotionally impossible in the language of the unsexual Martian people, yet filling a need for Michael, who is Martian only by thought. Biologically he is a man, and "the unsexual Martian _grok_ broadens to include the fullest and most intimate communication humanly possible, the very essence of life itself . . . revitalizing the archaic meaning of the Biblical _know_ as well as emphasizing the ambiguity of the Terran word _intercourse_."[18]

Stranger in a Strange Land is like an agar culture in which to plant _grok_ and let it grow; semantic symbols abound, not the least evidenced by the three names chosen for the messianic protagonist, but even the smallest of the symbols reenforces the theme of cultural and linguistic relativity in communication. One critic says, "Translated, 'Grok' is a cry of friendship,"[19] and another says, "The word was created by Robert A. Heinlein, dean of American science fiction writers . . . who has apparently read his Whorf well . . . in the thesis of

---

[17] Heinlein, p. 204.

[18] McNelly, p. 4.

[19] "The Publishing Scene," _Saturday Review_, XXX (March 18, 1967), p. 26.

linguistic relativity . . . that 'Love,' however extrapolated from whatever widely divergent culture, will find an identity of expression."[20] In addition to Whorf's theory of the relation between a culture's thought and its language, it can be added that Heinlein apparently read his Hayakawa as well. Characters in the book speak of "territories" and language "maps," and <u>grok</u> grows into the type of verbal signal that can span the prejudicial differences in cultural conditioning.[21]

Ethnocentrism is a basic factor in prejudice. Because our way is the best way, the theory says, and because all others are not like us, then all others are strange. Hayakawa focuses upon the word <u>all</u> in order to show how such generalization can build a semantic barrier between people. <u>All</u> individuals within any ethnic or cultural group are <u>not</u> alike--all Jews are not usurous, all Orientals are not philosophical, all Indians are not treacherous, all Frenchmen are not unpunctual, all Germans are not studious; and even cows, although they may look alike to a human, are all individuals. Hayakawa expresses this theory of faulty generalization as

---

[20] McNelly, p. 5.

[21] Heinlein no doubt had a reason for creating a word that sounds so unpleasant as <u>grok</u>; it is intended to symbolize a pleasant concept, and perhaps this phonetic-psychology is designed to affect the "hearing" of the reader as well as his thinking.

"Cow_1 is not Cow_2."[22] Communication, under such pre-conditioned cultural standards, is hampered from the start.

From the symbolic standpoint, however, this aspect of semantic evaluation has its own colorful place in a language. "Palefaces" are not referring to Indians when they say "Indian giver," and "Russian roulette" has nothing to do with the Soviet Union; anyone can "take French leave" or behave like a "Latin lover" or be as mysterious as a "Chinese puzzle." These expressions have "meaning" only in an American's view of those qualities as they appear in other cultures. Just as a Frenchman would probably miss the implications in "French leave," although he might understand the act, so Americans do not call themselves "palefaces" or "gringos" or "yanks," or refer to "the Yankee knowhow." It is for other cultures to judge us by their standards.

The language of cultural prejudice makes up the dialogue in Robert Nathan's "A Pride of Carrots,"[23] a short story written in the style of a play, with unlikely stage directions and asides from the author. In this "little masterpiece of spoofing . . . as a blithe satire on almost everything, technological rather than artistic values are involved."[24] That

---

[22]See the chapter entitled "Cow_1 Is Not Cow_2" in Hayakawa's *Language in Thought and Action*.

[23]Robert Nathan, "A Pride of Carrots," *Science Fiction Oddities*, pp. 169-202.

[24]*Ibid.*, p. 169 Editor's introduction.

it is a "spoof," if not discernible by the title, becomes obvious in the first action of the story as two American space travelers arrive--by parachute--on the planet Venus. The first encounter that Caudle and Potter have is with a "watch-gryphon" named Fido, who informs Caudle that it has seen him on television:

>   CAUDLE: Do you mean to say that our television reaches to . . . that you have . . . that . . . that there's television on Venus?
>   GRYPHON: Venus? What do you mean, Venus? You're from Venus. Up there. (He points.)
>   CAUDLE: But that's Earth.
>   GRYPHON: Nonsense . . . this is Earth. At least, we call it Earth. And we call that Venus. Apparently you call that Earth, and this Venus. Well . . . that's semantics for you. Silly, isn't it. What is your word for . . . for miscegenation?
>   CAUDLE: Why . . . inter-marriage, I suppose. Mésalliance.
>   GRYPHON: We call it cross-pollination. And what would you call a group of carrots?
>   CAUDLE: A bunch?
>   GRYPHON: Good heavens! A bunch? A pride of carrots! That is, of course, on this side of the border. And a gaggle of onions. But if you were on the other side . . . it would be an exaltation of onions, and a deceit of carrots. Semantics, you see.
>   CAUDLE (bemused): I see. I see.
>   GRYPHON (modestly): A charm of gryphons.
>   CAUDLE: You are a . . . gryphon, I take it?[25]

Fido and the Americans are joined by Fido's owner, the Secretary of the Interior, who arrives with his wife in a "crate of state" to welcome the spacemen. Edwin and Edwina are handsome carrots, and they courteously ask what the men

---

[25]Ibid., pp. 171-72. Ellipsis marks are not mine; they are used in the story.

would like for refreshment. The impulsive newsman Caudle starts to answer, but the more perceptive Potter interrupts with "Air! We've never eaten anything but air in our whole lives! . . . And water will do nicely." Edwina graciously asks if he wants it poured over him, or if he would prefer to stand in it. Officially welcomed, the men are escorted to the capital city, Carrotopolis, where Edwin must supervise a speech being written for him by "a talented young parsnip."

Meanwhile in Onionapolis, in the United Socialist Republic of Leeks and Onions, the Secretary, who is a large white onion named O'Dor, is angered to hear that the spacemen have landed in enemy territory instead of his own. He calls his aide, an humble leek:

> O'DOR: Exchanging insults with the carrots isn't going to bring these spacemen over to our own side . . . . We must get hold of their technical skill . . . before the carrots get it.
> LEEK: Yes, Little Father.
> O'DOR: It is ridiculous--is it not?--that we, who invented television, jet propulsion, the atom bomb, and the bicycle, should be deprived of these two men who could tell us how to use them . . . . Death to carrots! Strength to onions! . . . Bring to me those scientists from the planet they--erroneously--call Earth.[26]

O'Dor and his leek are making plans to seduce the earthmen with the charms of "a sweet little Spanish onion . . . no wrinkles . . . sweet and hot," when General Shallot enters and

---

[26]Ibid., p. 178.

addresses O'Dor as "comrade." O'Dor feels affronted:

>O'DOR: You <u>could</u> call me Excellency. Or Little Father.
>SHALLOT (proudly): I am a descendent of the garlics. A garlic does not call <u>anything</u> Excellency.
>O'DOR (hastily): <u>I</u> was only joking. Ha ha ha. Here we are all comrades! All excellencies . . . Little Fathers. Except Leeks.[27]

Back in Carrotopolis, Edwin and Edwina's crisp and tender teenage daughter, Alice, sits in the moonlight with a young carrot captain:

>ALICE: Do you love me?
>HERBERT: Madly.
>ALICE: Life is a bag of peat moss . . . . Love is so seasonal. I must ask Brian--the navy man Potter--if it's seasonal where he comes from.
>HERBERT (jealously): What would he know of love? He has no blossoms.
>ALICE: He must have something . . . . Love is so dull, Herbert. All those flies, everywhere you go.
>HERBERT: Bees, darling. Not flies--bees.
>ALICE (petulantly): What's the difference? They have wings.[28]

In Edwin's study, he and Potter discuss life, religion, politics. Asked why the onions are enemies, Edwin answers, "They want everyone to be round and white and onions. When as a matter of fact, the only possible thing for everyone to be-- if they're to have a decent kind of life--is long and crisp and carrots." He also explains why their television does not

---

[27]<u>Ibid.</u>, p. 181.
[28]<u>Ibid.</u>, p. 182.

extend to Potter's planet: "We broadcast to the insects, and even to the birds; but not, as a rule to the animal kingdom. Our experience with the rabbits, you know." And they speak of religion:

>   CAUDLE: Mysterious are the ways of the Lord. Having made man in His own image . . .
>   EDWIN: What?
>   CAUDLE: I said . . . The Lord having made man in His own image . . .
>   EDWIN: Why man, in particular?
>   CAUDLE: It says so. In Genesis 1:26.
>   EDWIN: Ah? But surely . . . the Lord, of whom you speak . . . and by whom, I imagine, you mean the Creator . . . must Himself be the root of all things--No?
>   CAUDLE: In a sense, of course . . .
>   EDWIN: Exactly. God is a root. You don't look in the least like a root. (Turning to his wife.) Does he, my dear? Do they?
>   EDWINA: Not all. He has no stalk. (Brightly to Potter.) Did you think you did?
>   Potter: I'm afraid I never gave it much thought, ma'am.[29]

Asking what Potter's wife is like, Edwina wonders how he can tell his own from the others:

>   POTTER: How do you tell one carrot from another?
>   EDWINA: No two carrots are alike. There are a thousand differences . . .
>   POTTER: To a carrot. It's the same with us.
>   EDWINA: Of course, my dear! Remember the rabbits? They all looked exactly the same--but they did seem able to recognize one another. And onions! They're just a faceless mob, as far as I'm concerned.[30]

---

[29] Ibid., p. 175.

[30] Ibid., p. 185.

Caudle and Potter conduct themselves with admirable decorum, and all seems well until a can of concentrated carrot juice rolls out of Potter's emergency ration pack. Then, crying "Cannibals!" Edwin summons the guards, who throw the two "dangerous vegetarians" into prison. But O'Dor and the leek, disguised as carrots, abduct the earthmen; Alice sacrifices her blossom to O'Dor in exchange for the lives of the men; and the faithless O'Dor orders his executioners, dressed as chefs, to put Alice in a soup.

"A Pride of Carrots" is a comedy in every line. The technology involved is cultural semantics, but a literary critic might disagree that it lacks artistry, if not literary value. Preliminary exposition of cultural environments is unnecessary, allowing the author to present his ideas in a shorter genre, because the reader already know the "cultural traits" of carrots and onions! The play form emphasizes speech, not actions, but the author's stage directions describe how the carrots wave their tassels in agreement, and the onions speak of their premier's "odor of authority." Here again, the message is between author and reader, with the earthmen as intermediaries. Even Caudel begins to ponder about his own narrow perspective as, in prison, he says, "You know, it makes you think. Suppose God *is* a root?"

Perspectives are cultural matters. Edwina says, in her own way, that "$Carrot_1$ is not $Carrot_2$," no matter how earthmen might view them. Hayakawa says that a language "map" might give a distorted view of the actual "territory" if both the speaker and the listener do not share the same perspectives and the same signals of "meaning." And the science of semantics says that the signals of communication--words, gestures, signs, colors, acts--that have "meaning" in one culture can communicate accurately to another culture only if the ethnic, personal, and cultural differences are properly recognized and respected.

CHAPTER IX

THE LANGUAGE OF THOUGHT CONTROL

Probably no field of linguistic study yields more variety of subdisciplines or more versatile applications to fictional literature than that of the relationship between language and culture. In a sense, all of linguistics is such a study, because language is a part of any cultural heritage. In a narrower sense, however, only a dead language has an identity apart from its speakers, and even languages now called "dead" were once part of a dynamic culture. A language becomes static only when it is no longer spoken by two native speakers, and a culture reaches a stage of stasis only when its people cease to exist. Living people, commonly united in a cultural group, will--and must--experience some type of evolutionary social change and some degree of linguistic change. Cultural anthropology, as a behavioral science, describes how people behave in social matters such as religion, government and marriage, including the ways in which they use language to express their thoughts. Linguistics, as a descriptive science, describes the way a language behaves in grammatical arrangement, vocabulary, and pronunciation as it is used by a people in expressing those thoughts.

People change, and their language changes. But does a

change in cultural attitudes cause people to begin speaking differently, or does a new trend in their speaking habits cause them to change their patterns of thought? Does a culture whose language has no distinction between _wife_ and _woman_ therefore think less highly of marriage? Or do the people value marriage so little that they have not bothered to make a linguistic distinction between one's own wife and women in general? Whether thought shapes language, or language shapes thought, it is generally agreed that there is a correlation between the language of a people and their outlook toward life.

In varying degrees, all creators of fictional languages reflect this relationship in their stories. The imaginary language is shaped to fit an imaginary people, and the character of the people is mirrored in the organization of the language created for them. This is an extremely interesting fact. Even writers who have virtually no knowledge of languages other than their own, or ones who admit to having no acquaintance with the actual study of cultural-linguistic relationship, still demonstrate this phenomenon in their imaginary languages. A simple fictional society usually has a simple language--that is, "simple" in the grammatical sense of being easily learned and spoken--and a complex society has a complex language. This observable fact that there is a correlation between the linguistic habits and the social attitudes of a people, both in reality and in fictional literature, is one that is given special attention by authors who have a didactic purpose in mind. All imaginary languages do not necessarily exhibit this type of correlation, or at least there is no reason for the author to stress it; authors who do, take special and unmistakable pains to identify those unusual attitudes or practices in the imaginary society that are expressed clearly in the unusual elements of their language. Once this emphasis has been noted--and a reader can hardly escape noticing it--the question arises as to chronology. Do the fictional people reflect their thought processes and behavior in the way that they have shaped their language, or do they react and think differently in certain areas of their life because specific, identifiable elements in their speech have given direction to their attitudes? Which change occurred first and caused a change in the other?

Franz Boas was concerned with linguistic and cultural relativity among indigenous American Indian tribes, but his interests lay primarily in examining the specialized vocabularies of occupational terms or weather conditions, and in recording the languages as an ethnological factor. It was his student Edward Sapir, later working with his own student, Benjamin Lee Whorf, who became interested in this language-culture relationship. Sapir and Whorf, working together with several American Indian tribes and their languages, began to arrive at an interesting theory when they noticed a direct correlation between certain grammatical elements in the language spoken by a tribe and the philosophy of thought within that culture.

Sometimes called the Sapir-Whorf theory, it is more often called the Whorfian Thesis, or Hypothesis, because of Whorf's later efforts on his own in solidifying and publishing his own conclusions. "Languages dissect nature in many different ways," Whorf says, "and all observers do not see the same picture of the universe unless their linguistic backgrounds are similar."[1] His famous study of the Hopi Indians examines the Hopi "timeless" language with its absence of verb tenses to denote an act completed or in progress or to be performed in the future, but with a sort of "psychological" time expressed by the speaker, who describes the act with expectation or memory or simple report.[2] The Hopi people themselves do not conceive of time, the duration of acts or events, in the same manner as the speakers of languages whose grammar does contain verb tenses, and the Hopis, therefore, have little regard for the actual passage of hours and days and years. Whorf's theory is that thoughts "march in step with purely grammatical facts."[3]

If, for example, a race of people had the physiological defect of being able to see only the color blue, they would not be able to formulate the rule that they see only blue, but

---

[1]Benjamin Lee Whorf, "Science and Linguistics," *Language and Culture: A Reader*, Patrick Gleeson and Nancy Wakefield, eds. (Columbus, Ohio: Charles E. Merrill Publishing Co., 1968), p. 45. This article is the authoritative expression of Whorf's thesis and first appeared in *Language, Thought and Reality* (MIT, 1956).

[2]Ibid., p. 49.   [3]Ibid., p. 43.

would see their color impressions only in terms of light and dark. Only by being able to see other colors could this hypothetical race be able to recognize that what they see is blue, says Whorf, and their language would lack color terms entirely. Their cultural traditions would then be built around symbols and habits that have no relation to colors. In simple terms, the Whorfian Thesis is that a people's "view of the world" is shaped by the language that they speak; language determines reality, or what is regarded as reality among its speakers.

Since Whorf's death in 1942, studies in the relationship between a language and its culture have been called "metalinguistic," in the sense of "going beyond" the forms of language to its manner of organizing experience.[4] Specialists in the field of metalinguistics agree that there is a relationship between the way a society thinks and the grammatical makeup of its language, but not all accept Whorf's hypothesis that it is language that shapes thought. Foremost spokesman among this group is Charles F. Hockett, professor of linguistics and anthropology at Cornell University, author of a book on structural grammar and many scholarly articles, and a theorist who develops and refines Whorf's ideas by analyzing the same types of language elements that Whorf himself

---

[4]Keesing, *Cultural Anthropology*, p. 376.

used.[5] There have always been dissenters who, in theory, disclaim the Whorfian Thesis, but Hockett illustrates his refinement with the same scholarly thoroughness that Whorf applied.

Claiming that Whorf based his theory on only Western languages, on American Indian languages in general and the Hopi language in particular, Hockett examined the same types of issues in Oriental languages, especially Chinese, to reach a conclusion whose importance is not to refute Whorf so much as to imply that the real causation may be more complex. Hockett's conclusion is that throughout history and its centuries of cultural changes, people have struggled against their inherited linguistic limitations, and when conditions have changed among a people, "speech habits were revised to accommodate those changes . . . . The causality is in all probability from 'philosophy of life' to language, rather than vice versa."[6]

---

[5]"Anti-Whorfian" will be used here to refer to the opposite of Whorf's theory, but it is not intended to refer to Hockett personally. Hockett's thesis is a refinement of Whorf's, not a refutation, and he offers it with hesitation. It is, however, the most scholarly treatment of anti-Whorfian argument.

Hockett states (in a letter dated March 13, 1971) that he had taken one course under Whorf and that there was never any controversy, either directly or indirectly, over the matter. Hockett says, also, that this subject has great interest to him, and that he is presently working on a book, to be published within the next two years, that will examine new dimensions to the language-culture-world view interaction.

[6]Charles F. Hockett, "Chinese Versus English: An Exploration of the Whorfian Theses (II)," Language and Culture: A Reader, pp. 132-33.

Language may influence thought (and, therefore, behavior), or thought may influence language. Because there is no solution to the question either way, even the most scholarly of debates could end in what one critic calls "a chicken-and-egg discussion."[7] Writers of fiction, however, suffer no frustration over this metalinguistic question; those that choose to deal with this aspect of language and culture simply begin with either the chicken or the egg. After examining a number of fictional treatments of the issue, a critic might conclude that both sides are valid, that the two together form a cycle of unending repetition: some new thing necessitates a social adaptation, and the language is adjusted to express the new concepts, which causes a new pattern of thought, which necessitates adding new dimensions to the grammar, and so on, ad infinitum. The circle analogy is convenient for an author because he can illustrate either side of the question without having to identify the original causation. His may be a society that controls its language or a society that is controlled by its language, but this dichotomy almost automatically becomes one of utopian-dystopian difference.

It has been mentioned previously, in various places throughout this study, that utopias--real utopias--reflect the kind of life that good men will develop for themselves by their own natural inclinations. Their naturally evolved

---

[7]Ornstein and Gage, p. 115.

language is one of convenience and utility, usually having many aesthetic terms and little or no profanity; its clarity allows the peaceful citizens to communicate with perfect understanding; and the utopian language itself is so uninteresting that the author is usually content to give a brief description of its grammatical structure, after which, the subject of language need not arise again. As a rule, a utopian imaginary language, even when a few actual words in the language occur throughout the book, is only incidental in a story and represents the type of language that the protagonist "quickly learns." The people are more important than their language in utopias.

For instance, Austin Tappan Wright's Islandia,[8] a bona fide utopia whose unstructured story rambles through more than two thousand manuscript pages, mentions the Islandian language only briefly in the second chapter and once later as an afterthought of the protagonist. The Islandians are a simple, unhurried, kind, idyllic people, and the protagonist, John Lang, speaks competent Islandian by the end of the second chapter (he arrives in Islandia at the beginning of the chapter). Lang describes the language as one having no gender, no declensions, no conjugations, no moods or tenses, but he does not explain how the people do communicate in such an uncomplicated language. The only Islandian words used in the book

---

[8]Austin Tappan Wright, Islandia (New York: Ferrar and Rinehart, Inc., 1942).

(except for personal names, which are even more descriptive than patronyms) are words meaning "love": *alia*, the love of family, clan, and country; *amia*, the platonic love for friends; *apia*, sexual love; and *ania*, the total spirit of love that encompasses all the others. Linguistic anthropology recognizes that this type of specialized vocabulary is indicative of an aspect of any culture which plays an important role in the life of the people. The Islandian people love, and their love is directed in ways that require special terms for each kind of love. These four words occur throughout the book, but after the second chapter, the Islandian language itself plays no role.

C. S. Lewis's planet of Malacandria is a utopia, but the function of the *hrossa* language is to illustrate how Ransom learned to speak it and not to reflect the character of the speakers. Lewis deals only in single words and their meanings, and he gives no indication of the overall structure of the language. There is some element of linguistic-cultural correlation, however, in the fact that each of the three species of creatures has its own language and its distinctive racial attitudes toward phonetic matters. The *hrossa* are a race of poets and musicians, the *séroni* are intellectuals and scientists, and the *pfifltriggi* are historians and artists. Ransom hears all three races speak the same language, although the two latter ones speak without the dialectical initial *h* that is characteristic of the *hrossa*. Only near the end of the story is he told by a <u>pfiltrig</u>, as he stands for a portrait being carved in stone, that the two other races have their own languages, but that they usually speak the <u>hrossa's</u> because it is more poetic. The <u>séroni</u>, Ransom is told, have "big-sounding names," the <u>hrossa</u> have "furry names," and the <u>pfifltriggi</u> have "hard-like-stone names."[9] The fictional Malacandrian, or Martian, language in <u>Out of the Silent Planet</u> is not illustrative of either Whorf's or Hockett's theory; it serves an entirely different purpose, as most utopian languages do.

To gather another set of previously mentioned comments, dystopias do not reflect the natural inclinations of good men. Anti-utopias are the result of social manipulation by intelligent but designing men who occupy the highest social or political status (though the ruling body may be of the second or third generation by the time the story takes place), and who can remain in power only through rigid control of the lower social strata that they have created. These leaders do not rule by physical force, but by social psychology; and their tool is language. Dystopian people and dystopian languages are always more interesting.

The languages created for dystopian purposes are almost always a form of English, so that they present no problem of comprehension to the ordinary reader, but they are composed of English elements that are reorganized and reshaped and re-

---

[9]Lewis, <u>Out of the Silent Planet</u>, p. 124.

valued in order to correspond with the attitudes of the particular dystopian society. Most prevalent and most significant is vocabulary, not in the creation of new words, but in the altered meaning which a familiar word takes on within the society; euphemisms abound, and the specialized vocabulary occurs in the area most emphasized in the society. ("Specialized vocabulary," in this case, might also refer to a complete absence of terminology familiar to the reader but for apparent reasons omitted from the language and the thoughts of the imaginary characters.) The language is sometimes a form of Basic English such as that in Boucher's "Barrier" (Chapter V); in this instance, the overriding purpose is to enforce stasis and standardization of all areas of society, and so the elimination of all irregularities in speech ("Who haves beed here today?") results in a Basic English. This imaginary, English-speaking society of the future falls on the Whorfian side of the cycle. The reshaping of social attitudes is still in its formative stages, the linguistic aspect being a problem that requires constant supervision; the new language patterns as set forth in the government treatise entitled "This Bees Speech" are, at this stage, rigidly enforced. The leaders apparently believe that any citizen who deviates in speech will also deviate in thought.

Less in evidence are fictional languages that are "anti-Whorfian." With the exception of unspectacular utopian speech, all dystopian languages technically belong to Whorf. All dystopian languages involve a measure of thought control, even if the actual enforcement of certain speech patterns is not a part of the book. When citizens of an obviously tyrannized society profess the belief that their world is near a state of perfection, and the language that they speak allows them neither to think nor utter contrary opinions, then it can be suspected that this situation is the successful result of an earlier period of language manipulation. However, the story takes place after the citizens have settled down comfortably in the language and become the type of citizens they were presumably intended to be, and the scope of action within the story involves a people whose language habits merely reflect their social habits and attitudes. Only in this type of imaginary society can Hockett be represented at all in the anti-utopian genre, but two of the "anti-utopian trilogy" are societies of this type.

Huxley's Brave New World,[10] with its goal of maintaining a static society has centered its attention on destroying all traces of family life. The word *mother* exists only as an obscenity, and there is no reference to any other familial relationship. Families, in fact, do not exist in the social program; babies are produced in governmentally controlled test tubes, prenatally conditioned to their predetermined social class (Alpha, Beta, Gamma, Delta, or Epsilon), and

---

[10]Aldous Huxley, Brave New World (New York:Harper and Brothers, 1932).

their future occupations (future rocket ship mechanics are developed upside-down). The people speak English, but where their language most reflects their view of life is not in such practical matters as test-tube babies, but in the emotional and psychological implications that usually accompany family life--love, sex, companionship, marital fidelity, child-rearing, religion. All male-female relationships are aimed at preventing personal attachments, religion is of the state-sponsored variety, and the god is Ford. Outside of single words or phrases relating to specific episodes, the most revealing aspect of language-culture correlation is found in the conversation of the aphorism-quoting characters. "Promiscuity is Virtue," one girl reminds another who has been seeing too much of the same male friend; in hygiene, "Cleanliness is Fordliness"; and profanity is "Ford in Flivver!"

An outstanding example of mathematical language reflecting a mathematical culture is found in Zamiatin's We,[11] the first modern anti-utopian novel, and one whose literary and linguistic devices have occurred with surprising frequency in almost every subsequent work in the genre since We was first published in 1924. This future world dates itself A. T. (After Tables), its citizens are called Numbers, and its view of the world is mathematically geometric; emotions are expressed as "round," "square," and "triangular." The protagonist, D-503,

---

[11]Eugene Zamiatin, We (New York: E. P. Dutton and Company, 1924).

is a mathematician who works on a rocket ship, reads mathematical tables for light reading, and has for years been the regular "sexual ticket Number" of the plump and naive O-90. All she-Numbers and he-Numbers live in glass-walled dormitories, as an inducement to "togetherness," and the only problem D-503 has encountered when the story begins is with an obsession of O-90's. She desperately wants a baby, but her request has been repeatedly denied because she is several centimeters short of the maternal norm. Because of his thoroughly analytic and logical mind, D-503 can solve "mathematical-moral problems" such as this, but his mind is confronted with an emotional "factor unknown" when he meets an alluring but unorthodox she-Number named I-330, who is a member of a revolutionary group. She looks at him "with X in her eyes," embroils him in a plot to overthrow the government, and thus causes him to develop the type of fanciful thoughts that are believed to be a form of "epilepsy." D-503 knows that "it is the duty of every loyal Number to report to the Guardians any act of epilepsy," and so he dutifully reports to the medical authorities for a cure of his malady:

> "What is wrong with me? Am I out of tune?"
> "Yes, it is too bad. Apparently a soul has formed in you."
> A soul? That strange, ancient word that was forgotten long ago . . . .
> "Is it . . . v-very dangerous?" I stuttered.
> "Incurable," was the reply . . . "the simple thing is to operate. Simply extirpate the center for fancy.

> Only surgery can help here, only surgery; it might even help us prevent an epidemic.[12]

However, D-503 delays his operation and begins to live a life "distorted by epilepsy, bombarded with X-factors with no clear equations," until the state publicly announces a breakthrough in the discovery of a "miserable little knot in the lower region of the frontal lobe of the brain" that is the center of fancy, and thus the cause of epilepsy. Numbers rush forward for the operation, which is, in effect, a mass lobotomy; the state later announces that its goal has been achieved--a perfect society, "a perfect world of humanized machines and mechanized humans."[13]

It is recognized in We, as in almost every story of this type, that human beings are malleable only to a point. Physiological and psychological needs are provided for, but in a means least destructive and most advantageous to the state. Sexual drive is utilized for state purposes or expended in harmless social activity or, as in We, regarded as a "sexual commodity." One other area that is rarely omitted is religion. Human beings apparently have the need to worship, and the state provides them a god--We's Well-Doer, Brave New World's Ford, 1984's Big Brother--and semantically canonizes the members of its law enforcement agency. D-503 and the other Numbers in this world look with reverence upon the Guardian Angels--Guardians, for short--and one of the

---

[12]Ibid., p. 84.   [13]Ibid., p. 166.

Guardians' functions is to conduct on-the-spot "confessionals" when a citizen looks suspiciously preoccupied. Thus, with religious idea-associations, the state can effect a holy reverence toward many acts and agencies that are far from holy.

The Newspeak language in Orwell's <u>1984</u> is probably the world's best known fictional, imaginary language. Because so much scholarly attention has already been devoted to it over the past two decades, Newspeak will be given less attention here than it deserves. As illustrated in the progress of the novel and explained by Orwell in the appendix "The Principles of Newspeak," it is a deliberately created language designed to bind and control the thought processes of its citizens. One of the characters, Syme, is a lexicographer currently working on the eleventh revised edition of the Newspeak dictionary, and Syme becomes the spokesman who describes the goals and inner workings of the constantly revised state language. Orwell, however, in his appendix, gives a nutshell analysis of the aims of the B vocabulary, which is entirely political in purpose:

> The purpose of Newspeak was not only to provide a medium of expression for the world-view and mental habits proper to the devotees of Ingsoc, but to make all other modes of thought impossible . . . . Newspeak was designed not to extend but to diminish the range of thought, and this purpose was indirectly assisted by cutting the choice of words down to a minimum . . . . The B vocabulary consisted of words which had been deliberately constructed for political purposes; words which not only had in every case a political implication, but were intended to impose a

desirable mental attitude upon the person using them . . . .
In Newspeak it was seldom possible to follow a heretical
thought further than the perception that it was heretical;
beyond that point the necessary words were nonexistent.[14]

One indispensable B vocabulary word is doublethink--both a noun and a verb--which indicates a citizen's ability to conceive of two opposites both as truth, and to believe wholeheartedly whichever one that is designated as true at any given moment. Another is crimestop, which refers to a sort of mental barricade that a citizen must throw up to stop himself short of any thought that is heretical (an impossibility, of course, since he must know that the thought he is about to think is heretical before he can take measures to stop himself from thinking it). A third word, crimethink, is the most versatile of all, since it becomes a substitute for any thought which is heretical in nature and therefore must not, and cannot, be expressed. (It might be noticed that crime against the state is called "heresy," not "treason.")

Orwell died shortly after completing 1984. He knew it was his last book, and so he apparently poured into it many of the theories already contained in his treatises on politics and the English language (his most famous is entitled "Politics and the English Language"). Believing that the deterioration of the English language would be instrumental in the decay of government, Orwell's fictional Newspeak is his

---

[14]Orwell, 1984, pp. 246 and 249.

illustration of how such a decay could take place. In a recent experiment at MIT's Computation Center, three students programed an IBM 7094 computer with Newspeak words contained in 1984 and, via a 1052 console, attempted to translate passages into Newspeak. Finding that selections from Orwell's other writings, which are political in nature, provided the best copy, they obtained some illuminating results. Here are a few examples:

What I have most wanted to do throughout the past ten years is to make political writing into an art. My starting point is always a feeling of partisanship, a sense of injustice.	What I have doubleplus wanted through ten anteyears is to make politwrite good form. My startfeel is always crimethink.
When I sit down to write a book, I do not say to myself, "I am going to produce a work of art."	When I start to bookwrite I do not selfspeak I will make a good form.
But I could not do the work of writing a book, or even a long magazine article, if it were not also an aesthetic experience.	But I could not bookwrite or even magwrite longwise if it was not also bellyfeel.
I am not able, and I do not want, completely to abandon the world-view that I acquired in childhood.	I cannot, and unwant to fullwise drop the oldthink I getted in plusyoung.
The job is to reconcile my ingrained likes and dislikes with the essentially public, nonindividual activities that this age forces on all of us.	The job is to rekcile my intrabuilded goodfeels and ungoodfeels with the mostwise unselful acts the nowtime onputs everybody.[15]

---

[15] Joseph Foley and James Ayer, "Orwell in English and Newspeak: A Computer Translation," College Composition and Communication, XVII (February 1966), 17-18. The Orwell selections were taken from his "Why I Write."

These selections in "Newspeak perversion" not only prove Newspeak a speakable language, but they illustrate the effectiveness of the language in rendering unutterable certain heretical thoughts; "the tenuousness of human freedom, the vulnerability of the will, and the genuine power of the scientist."[16]

A most unusual and richly Whorfian book is Jack Vance's The Languages of Pao.[17] Pao is a planet, and the Paonese people are

> a simple uncomplicated people . . . without religion or cult . . . . The language of Pao was . . . molded into peculiar forms. The Paonese sentence did not so much describe an act as it presented a picture of a situation. There were no verbs, no adjectives; no formal word comparison such as good, better best.[18]

Paonese is only one of the eight languages in this book, but Paonese and the Paonese people provide both a starting point and a conclusion, as they are manipulated and subliminally directed for the length of the story. The simplicity and pastoral nature of the Paonese people make them prey to a potential dictator whose plans to assume control of both the planet of Pao and its people directly involve language as a controlling factor. The theme of this book is thought control

---

[16]Anthony Burgess, The Novel Now (New York: W. W. Norton and Co., Inc., 1967), p. 44.

[17]Jack Vance, The Languages of Pao (New York: Ace Books, Inc., 1958).

[18]Ibid., p. 6.

through language, and it is the internal organization of each language that is important, not actual words written in an imaginary tongue. The scope is larger than single words or single sentences, the theme is linguistics, and the major characters are linguists.

The protagonist, Beran, is a child when the story begins, carefully nurtured as the future hereditary ruler of Pao. He is taken, at age nine, to the planet of Breakness, to Breakness Institute, the College of Comparative Culture, to study, he is told, "the races of the universe, their similarities and differences, their languages and basic urges, the specific symbols by which you can influence them."[19] He receives instruction:

> "Now," said Fanchiel briskly, "to the language of Breakness."
> . . . Beran's obstinacy returned. "Why can't we speak Paonese?"
> Fanchiel explained patiently. "You will be required to learn a great deal that you could not understand if I taught in Paonese."
> "I understand you now," muttered Beran.
> "Because we are discussing the most general ideas. Each language is a special tool, with a particular capability. It is more than a means of communication, it is a system of thought. . . . Think of a language as the contour of a watershed, stopping flow in certain directions, channeling it into others. Language controls the mechanism of your mind. When people speak different languages, their minds work differently and they act differently. . . . The question arises: does the language provoke or merely reflect the eccentricity? Which came first: The language or the conduct?[20]

---

[19]Ibid., p. 44.   [20]Ibid., p. 45-46.

Men of the planet Breakness are scientists, linguists, wizards, intelligentsia, psychologists who "sell the workings of their mind," and they sell their skills with professional impartiality. While they protect and educate the young prince Beran, they also serve the usurper of Beran's throne, his own uncle, who asks for advice on how he can spur the laconic Paonese into activity. He is told by Palafox, a Breakness advisor, that the first step is to persuade the amenable Paonese to become fighters:

> "We must alter the mental framework of the Paonese people--a certain proportion of them, at least--which is most easily achieved by altering the language. . . . Words are tools. Language is a pattern, and defines the way the word-tools are used."
> Bustamonte was eying Palafox sidelong. "How can this theory be applied practically? Do you have a definite detailed plan?"
> "This is what must be done. . . . The people of this area will be persuaded to the use of a new language. That is the extent of the effort. Presently they will produce warriors in profusion. . . . Paonese is a passive, dispassionate language. A people speaking Paonese, theoretically, ought to be docile, passive, without strong personality development--in fact, exactly as the Paonese people are. The new language will be based on the contrast and comparison of strength, with a grammar simple and direct. To illustrate, consider the sentence, "The farmer chops down a tree." (Literally rendered from the Paonese in which the two men spoke, the sentence was: "Farmer <u>in state of exertion</u>; axe <u>agency</u>; tree <u>in state of subjection to attack</u>.") In the new language the sentence becomes: "The farmer overcomes the inertia of the axe; the axe breaks asunder the resistance of tree." Or perhaps: "The farmer vanquishes the tree, using the weapon-instrument of the axe."[21]

---

[21]<u>Ibid</u>., pp. 55-57.

The linguistic psychology of this proposed language includes a syllabary rich in effort-producing gutturals and hard vowels; vocabulary is based on key-words making synonymous key ideas such as <u>pleasure</u> and <u>overcoming a resistance</u>, <u>relaxation</u> and <u>shame</u>, <u>out-worlder</u> and <u>rival</u>. Within the estimated twenty years for cultural attitudes to merge with these linguistic patterns, the Paonese should be fierce fighters, taking pleasure in their battles, always in action, and possessive of their own territory.

To this warrior-producing language, so promising in theory, are added two more systems, one with a grammar extravagantly complicated, but consistent and logical, designed to produce industrialists and manufacturers; and another, "a symmetrical language . . . with elaborate honorifics to teach hypocrisy, a vocabulary rich in homophones to facilitate ambiguity, a syntax of reflection" to produce a corps of merchants and traders. Each language will be isolated from the others, and each language enclave should produce its own type of Paonese people, Palafox explains:

> "All these languages will make use of semantic assistance. To the military segment, a 'successful man' will be synonymous with 'winner of a fierce contest,' To the industrialists, it will mean 'efficient fabricator." To the traders, it equates with "a person irresistibly persuasive.' Such influences will pervade each of the languages. Naturally they will not act with equal force upon each individual, but the mass action must be decisive."

"Marvelous!" cried Bustamonte, completely won over. "This is human engineering indeed!"[22]

The three proposed languages, named Valiant, Technicant, and Cogitant, are set up in language enclaves on Pao, and years pass. The young Beran, at seventeen, is denied in his request to return to his native Pao, but quite by accident he meets a group of young Paonese men brought to Breakness to study languages. These apprentice linguists are to be trained as the elite, the supervisors of all the language enclaves on their planet and, as Interpreters, they are to be educated in the "science of dynamic linguistics." Using a fictitious name, Beran successfully enrolls with the group, hoping to be returned with them at the end of their course of study. During the year, the young men playfully invent a language of their own, "a bastard mish-mash of a language" that they call Pastiche and claim as the characteristic tongue of the Interpreters, vying for fluency in their invented language.

Beran's scheme works. He is returned to Pao, but as more years pass, he finds that the languages have been too successful. The Paonese, once a united and peaceful people, are not only separated into divergent language groups, but they are becoming a race of belligerent, hypocritical, ultra-competetive swaggerers. And the "mish-mash" Pastiche becomes more and more useful for intercommunication when Interpreters cannot be

---

[22]Ibid., pp. 57-58.

present. Beran discovers that the Valiant warriors appear more docile when they hear their native Paonese language and, when he regains his rightful place as ruler of Pao, one of his first decrees is that Paonese subjects be taught in the Paonese language. The Valiants, Technicants, and Cogitants are no longer a unified people, Beran realizes, when he hears a Valiant warrior say "you Paonese." Since language was the impetus of the division, language may also reunite the people; Beran establishes Pastiche, which began as a student joke, as the official language of Pao: Pastiche--composite of Breakness, Cogitant, Technicant, Valiant, Paonese. "Pastiche--the language of service. In twenty years, everyone will speak Pastiche. It will fertilize the old minds, shape the new minds. What kind of world will Pao be then?"[23]

The Languages of Pao is not a book about language; it is a book built by language, an exposition of dynamic linguistics that illustrates the potential impact of linguistic patterns upon behavioral patterns.[24] It, like 1984, is entirely Whorfian in theme, but fictional treatments of thought control through language are more predictable, more provable, and less theoretical than actual, scholarly debates on the subject.

---

[23]Ibid., p. 157.

[24]Although this book illustrates Whorf's theory, Vance disclaims any intention to do so. Vance says, "I intended the book not as an hortatory tract, but as the development of an interesting concept, which may or may not be valid." (Letter dated January 25, 1971.)

Writers can make their characters behave according to plan, but somehow, even to the uninitiated layman, it seems improbable that real human beings would accept an enforced new language, much less change their basic attitudes in accordance with a new set of linguistic values. Even Edward Sapir, co-founder of the Whorfian Thesis, stated that "language is probably the . . . most massively resistant of all social phenomena."[25] An analytic reader might wonder, in addition, how much faith writers of fiction have in the theory that they illustrate in action, since the protagonist in virtually every such story is one who rebels against its forces. Winston Smith, in Orwell's story, has an instinctive resistance against what the government claims is true; he is conquered, but through torture and not through subliminal control.

If it were true that the language spoken by a people has shaped the thought of that people, then it could also be asked how such a language came into being if it were not created by a people who already thought that way. All facts of scientific history point to the presence of people first, and language later. Of course, language is one of the areas of human life that cannot be governed by logic, but the human animal is no less subject to instinctive knowledge and reaction than is the beast. Human nature cannot be ignored, even in fiction, and it seems significant that protagonists are always unusual in

---

[25] Quoted in Keesing, p. 374.

relation to the society they represent; they are a little more rational, even if their IQ is average, and they are possessed of a greater degree of reasoning power, or instinctive knowledge, or whatever the nature of that quality that causes them not to behave with sheep-like obedience. This fact is most observable in anti-utopian works, when the protagonist has grown up under the identical conditions as the rest of society, and yet he knows that all is not right. And he is not alone; works of anti-utopian fiction invariably include a group of "outlaws" who have already identified the flaws in this "ideal" society and withdrawn because of them.

Ayn Rand unites these elements of dystopian fiction in the language of Anthem,[26] a short novel whose plot, theme, and message revolve around the absence of one word. Anthem is a narrative, and the protagonist introduces himself:

> Our name is Equality 7-2521, as it is written on the iron bracelet which all men wear on their left wrists with their names upon it. We are twenty-one years old. We are six feet tall, and this a burden, for there are not many men who are six feet tall. Ever have the Teachers and the Leaders pointed to us and frowned and said: "There is evil in your bones, Equality 7-2521, for your body has grown beyond the bodies of your brothers." But we cannot change our bones nor our body.
> We were born with a curse. . . . We strive to be like all our brother men, for all men must be alike.[27]

---

[26] Ayn Rand, Anthem (New York: The New American Library, Inc., 1946). Rand outlined this story as a play, when she was sixteen and still living in her native Russia. Because political plays could not be published in Russia, it lay dormant until 1937, after her migration to the United States, when she recast it as a novel.

[27] Ibid., p. 13.

This young man has, first, committed the sin of growing taller than his friends, and, at the time when vocations are assigned, he commits the Sin of Preference by preferring to be a scholar; for punishment, he is assigned to be a street sweeper for the rest of his life.

He calls himself "we" because there is no other word. A classmate "were a pale boy, a sickly lad, and sometimes they are stricken with convulsions, when their mouth froths and their eyes turn white."[28] There are, in fact, no singular pronouns or verb forms in the language. The narrator speaks the language of his people, and he expresses himself adequately until he falls in love. Finally, he and the girl find an opportunity to speak together:

> "You are beautiful, Liberty 5-3000."
> Their face did not move and they did not avert their eyes. Only their eyes grew wider, and there was triumph in their eyes, and it was not triumph over us, but over things we could not guess.
> Then they asked:
> "What is your name?"
> "Equality 7-2521," we answered.
> "You are not one of our brothers, Equality 7-2521, for we do not wish you to be."
> We cannot say what they meant, for there are no words for their meaning, but we know it without words and we knew it then.
> "No," we answered, "nor are you one of our sisters."[29]

There are many Sins in this world, but there is only one Crime. That offense, the only offense punishable by death, is the crime of uttering the Unspeakable Word. No one seems to

---

[28]Ibid., p. 26.   [29]Ibid., pp. 43-44.

know what that unspeakable word is, but the protagonist, as a child, had once witnessed a man put to death for that offense after having his tongue torn out. As the Transgressor was dying, their eyes met and "it seemed as if those eyes were begging us to gather that word and not to let it go from us and from the earth. But the flames rose and we could not guess the word."[30]

The two lovers meet clandestinely, until the young man is banished by the Council for his presumptuousness in inventing electrical current. As the girl follows him into the Uncharted Forest outside the city, they begin life together as exiles. But he is bothered:

> . . . These joys belong to us alone, they come from us alone, they bear no relation to our brothers, and they do not concern our brothers in any way. Thus do we wonder. . . . There is some error, one frightful error, in the thinking of men. What is that error? We do not know, but the knowledge struggles within us, struggles to be born.
> Today, the Golden One stopped suddenly and said: "We love you."
> But then they frowned and shook their head and looked at us helplessly.
> "No," they whispered, "that is not what we wished to say."
> They were silent, then they spoke slowly, and their words were halting, like the words of a child learning to speak for the first time:
> "We are one . . . alone . . . and only . . . and we love you who are one . . . alone . . . and only."
> We looked into each other's eyes and we knew that the breath of a miracle had touched us, and fled, and left us groping vainly.
> And we felt torn, torn for some word we could not find.[31]

---

[30] Ibid., p. 53.   [31] Ibid., pp. 98-99.

In <u>Anthem</u>'s world of the future, "<u>I</u> is the root of all evil, or so the altruistic collectivists declare. . . . The word <u>I</u> has disappeared from men's language, . . . having destroyed the independent mind through the destruction of individualizing words."[32] But Equality 7-2521 finds the word--in an ancient house left by forgotten men, in a library still intact, in an ancient book:

> It was when I read the first of the books I found in my house that I saw the word "I." And when I understood this word, the book fell from my hands, and I wept, I who had never known tears.
> . . . .
> I AM. I THINK. I WILL.
> My hand . . . My spirit . . . My sky . . . My forest . . . This earth of mine. . . .
> What must I say besides? These are the words. This is the answer.[33]

In style and form, <u>Anthem</u> is closer to poetry than to prose. The diction of the narrator-protagonist is simple, without contractions or other economy of effort, almost archaic at times. Most striking is the absence of <u>I</u>:

> The hero's struggle to identify and name the concept of "I" is developed with such tension that when, after pages of "we," one sees the opening line of the climactic chapter, the emotional experience is one of unsurpassing violence and power:
> "I AM. I THINK. I WILL."[34]

---

[32]Nathaniel Branden, <u>Who Is Ayn Rand?</u> (New York: Random House, Inc., 1962), p. 111.

[33]Rand, <u>Anthem</u>, pp. 114 and 108.   [34]Branden, p. 113.

The purpose of *Anthem* is to expose a philosophy, not to illustrate a language; but the philosophy is best illustrated through language, the language of a totally collectivized society whose altruistic aims have resulted in the elimination of all individualizing acts and words.[35] In *Anthem*, the language of this society is, in all likelihood, not a naturally evolved language. It is apparent in *Anthem*, as in other books of this type, that man controls his language and not vice versa. If a concept is present in the human mind, it will find a means of expression; unhampered, man will fashion his language into an efficient tool, but if his language is by some means distorted and constricted and semantically misconstrued, then his means of expression is frustrated--but his mind nevertheless continues to function. *Anthem*'s hero has the concept of "ego" in his emotions long before he realizes that he needs a word to express it, just as *1984*'s Winston Smith knows that two and two do not make five, no matter what the government says. Had Equality 7-2521 never found the ancient books, he still would probably have created his own word for expressing his individuality. The word probably would not have sounded like *I*, but it would have nevertheless signified "ego." And that is the way a language begins.

---

[35]There are inconsistencies in this language. It seems that the words *one* and *alone* should not be known, and once (on p. 102) the word *was* occurs. This is undoubtedly an oversight on the author's part, but these inconsistencies are not detrimental to the overall effect.

When the language-culture relationship is emphasized in fantasy fiction, the work automatically becomes utopian or anti-utopian. Utopias occur on the anti-Whorfian side of the cycle, and anti-utopias on the Whorf side.[36] The latter, in which language has been instrumental in producing a society that thinks according to plan, centers around a protagonist who attempts to break both the cultural and linguistic molds into which his life has been forced. But he does not succeed.

With one exception, the protagonist in anti-utopian works--I have personally encountered over one hundred stories in this genre--is defeated by the system. <u>Anthem</u> is the only anti-utopia I have ever found that has a happy ending.

---

[36] One point that was purposely not brought up until now is this: Whorf formed his theory primarily on his studies of the Hopis, but in explaining it, he used the analogy of the hypothetical race who could see only the color blue. He begins, "For instance, if a race of people had the physiological defect of being able to see only the color blue . . . ," (p. 41). It is interesting that Whorf, in attempting to prove that thoughts begin with language, begins his explanation, not with language, but with a physical defect.

CONCLUSION

It would be misleading to claim that linguistic principles, as found in science fiction-fantasy, are "valid," but it is in order to observe that science-fictional languages do assume interesting shapes. The purpose of this study, originally, was to test certain theories as applied to hypothetical, imaginary languages, simply to see if they had enough systematic organization to be speakable. As the study progressed, other areas of linguistics presented themselves as criteria when a particular work seems to demand a standard other than speakability. Some literary selections contain a language, or several languages, that could have been examined under almost every area of linguistic study included here, but they were placed arbitrarily under the area they most clearly exemplify. Other selections, not included within the study itself (but listed in the bibliography), are an entertaining and interesting miscellany. Some of these selections contain poetry or only small portions of a fictional language, and others would have been included within the study had they been discovered earlier.

Science fiction and fantasy literature has often been called a literature of communication. This study has centered upon only one medium of communication--language--often to the exclusion of the purpose intended by the authors. Science fiction has more than its share of novice writers who produce "potboilers" and what are termed derogatorily as "space operas" (not referring to the Swedish "Space Opera," which is actually an opera about space, but to a sort of "outer space soap opera.") Stories of this type are usually purely escape fiction with dubious literary value, but the "literature of communication" is concerned almost entirely with communicating ideas, often with didactic purpose. When these ideas are presented through the medium of language, such as in <u>1984</u> and "Barrier" and <u>The Languages of Pao</u>, then literary criticism could hardly be undertaken without linguistics as a major examining factor. This fact is obvious, but it is hoped that this study has introduced new dimensions to linguistic criticism which, as an adjunct to literary criticism, helps bring to light certain literary factors which would otherwise remain undiscovered.

De Camp's "Wheels of If" could well be a simple escape story without the knowledge of historical linguistics to illuminate the scholarship involved in contriving a plot which bypasses every important event in the development of the English language; the rather odd speech of the characters could be simply entertaining without the realization that it is actually what our English language might have become had the events of history happened differently. Similarly, <u>A Clockwork Orange</u> can be read and enjoyed and criticized without the application of linguistics; but when linguistics can help to identify the origins of the unique Nadsat jargon in which the book is written, both the literary style and the book's message gain in power. The Newspeak in <u>1984</u>, had Orwell not considered it a factor vital enough to explicate himself, would have been of great linguistic interest, and there is no doubt that the grammatical system of Newspeak parallels and enforces the theme of the entire book.

In addition to these broad ways in which specific areas of linguistics can be applied in literary criticism, it is a matter of simple pleasure for a reader who is interested in language to be alert to the linguistic games and puzzles that are available in science fiction literature. "Fictionalized shop talk" can also be read with enjoyment, and perhaps linguists would find challenges in Tolkien's <u>The Lord of the Ring</u> trilogy, just as analysis of the Ent language provided for this study. A polyglot linguist who knows Spanish, Russian, and German might investigate the "langue earthly" in Boucher's "Barrier" for the appropriate inflections in each language (an investigation which was not attempted here), or have the phonetic and grammatical skills to match de Camp's construction of the interplanetary pidgin, Intermundos.

In addition to literary criticism and personal challenge, there are linguistic issues appearing only in this type of literature that are important for their speculative value. The possibility of inter-species communication has been a serious object of national interest since 1962, when a contract was awarded by the National Aeronautics and Space Administration for "Project Dolphin."[1] In charge of the project is Dr. John Lilly, a neurophysiologist and a noted authority on the mammal, who was awarded the contract for basic research "on the feasibility and methodology for establishing communications between man and other species."[2] Notice that the wording is not "man and dolphin," but "man and other species":

> . . . It is obvious that before our spacemen confront alien beings on a distant planet, we must learn the fundamentals of developing communication with a non-human but intelligent species . . . on earth. . . . [The dolphin language] needs the skills of the radio astronomer in extracting signals from noise, and then the work of thelinguist, and, perhaps, the cryptographer. It could well be, if the dolphin studies are correct, that we have right here on earth another intelligent race that is even more alien than some we might encounter in space.[3]

Not only is there "Project Dolphin," but other projects are investigating forms of nonverbal communication among earth's species, such as the antenna-speech of ants and the gyrations of bees. Such studies are not speculation; they are the result of speculation. The United States government has already taken

---

[1] Vincent H. Gaddis, "The New Science of Space Speech," *Worlds of Tomorrow*, I (August, 1963), 115-123. This article, although it lacks the developments of the past eight years, summarizes and examines the many projects in which both our government and private research foundations are attempting to devise new means of communication with other species. It contains, in addition, some interesting documentation concerning unexplained signals that have been received by radio waves since early in 1924, including the famous "face message."

[2] *Ibid.*, pp. 17-18.

[3] *Ibid.*, p. 18.

into consideration that alien beings might communicate in ways impossible for human beings, but in order to prepare for any contingency, it must operate on speculations that sound as if they come directly from a science fiction story! And the fact is that, although government communications experts may not attribute their ideas to a fiction story, the same ideas have probably already appeared to the point of triteness in science fiction. Science fiction is a literature of scientific hypothesis, but

> science fiction did not invent speculative thinking; it was quite the other way round. . . . Now, some of the best story plots are going into reports by research and development men for the government, the armed services, the big corporations, and such novelties in our scheme of things as the Rand Corporation. What part of this thinking is not channeled into governmental or industrial secrecy is as likely to appear in essay form in a serious journal as in adventure trappings in the magazines.[4]

It is probably assumed that the "science" concerned in science fictional speculation is one of the physical sciences--physics, meteorology, astronomy, or chemistry--but there are other sciences that also speculate through this medium. Linguistics is belatedly joining into hypothetical suggestions that are firmly based upon knowledge in the field and that may be as valuable as any that the physical sciences have to offer.

Specifically, using examples that are contained within the selections in this study, here are a few of the hypothetical

---

[4] Judith Merril, "Summation: The Year in S-F," 6th Annual Edition of the Year's Best S-F, pp. 374-75.

suggestions that pertain to inter-species communication: in Boucher's "Barrier" is suggested that there is probably no "Martian language" or "Venusian language"; a planet of such size is more likely to have many languages, as our planet does, which may be unintelligible to each other. If our scientists should ever successfully establish communication with a race of alien peoples, then fail to achieve the same results with a second group, this hypothesis could provide an explanation for the failure and an incentive for beginning the decipherment of a second alien language. The Intermundos in de Camp's "New Arcadia" presents the theory that alien physiognamy may differ to such a degree that neither species is physically able to speak the language of the other; in this event, an intermediate language could be based upon whichever phonemes the species have in common, with allowances for interchangeable phonemes. Even Nathan's carrots offer an idea, though not a revolutionary one. (Martians *might* have tassels to wave, instead of hands.) Heinlein's concept of "grok" could have applications of infinite variety, since alien species could share many of our bodily functions or environmental appurtenances, but ignoring the possible differences in inter-cultural implications could create more problems than it could rectify. Inversely, as illustrated with Asimov's telepathic "color patch" aliens, our most basic facts of life might be misunderstood or misinterpreted by another race with different biological functions or aesthetic values.

Writers of science fiction-fantasy have serious ideas to present, but one characteristic of the genre is that it can laugh at itself while presenting them. Charles F. Hockett has written one of "the only two popularizations of technical linguistics"[5] in science fiction, and while his subject matter is every bit as scholarly as his "anti-Whorfian" theories, his manner of presenting it is truly delightful. He begins:

> An agent of the Galactic Federation, sent to Earth to case the joint secretly for either friendly or inimical purposes, could do a good deal worse than to make a survey of the scientific terms that appear, quite casually, in contemporary science fiction. . . . If the agent's sole aim were to measure our technological potential, science fiction would be of no great help. But if he also wanted to determine the <u>degree of general technological readiness</u> of the whole population . . . then the suggested survey would be of considerable value.[6]

It is Hockett's observation that linguistics, of all the sciences, is the one area of communication that might most mislead the alien spy; "an occasional term of modern linguistics turns up from time to time in science fiction: 'phoneme,' in particular, is a word to conjure with just as much as is 'transistor' or 'cybernetics.'"[7] But when a writer does use a linguistic term "such as phonemes, morphemes, intonations,

---

[5]Ornstein and Gage, p. 200.

[6]Charles F. Hockett, "How to Learn Martian," <u>Astounding Science Fiction</u>, LV (May, 1955), 97. (Now called <u>Analog</u>.)

[7]<u>Ibid</u>., p. 98.

immediate constituents, the impact of language on culture, and the like," he must stop and explain it to the reader, thereby signaling to the alien that the general public knows little or nothing about the subject. Linguists are "Johnny-come-latelies," Hockett says, and have done little to educate the public in man's most important form of communication--language.

Hockett then takes the reader on a make-believe journey to Mars and allows him to observe the proceedings as the ship's xenologist, Ferdinand Edward Leonard, B. A., M. A., Ph.D., M. D., X. D. ("who is about as chock full of modern anthropological, linguistic, communicative, engineering, psychiatric, and biological training as one skin can be stuffed with") sits down with a Martian and attempts to decipher the Martian's language. The article, from this point on, is pure linguistics, never sparing the reader from technical terms and scholarly interpretations. Assuming that the sounds Marty the Martian makes are really language, and not just Martian throat-clearing, he says, the language can be deciphered; Hockett illustrates, step by step, exactly how it can be done. Marty helps ("closing his middle eye--apparently the gesture of assent"), and the xenologist collects phonetic information about the Martian's language (not "the Martian language.") Hockett's article closes with a listing of some possible means of intelligent communication other than verbal language, and he expresses concern about the linguistic training that is being given to xenologists (apparently Hockett's parallel to the "exolinguists" of this study) for possible future use.

Hockett's concern for the state of linguistic ignorance on the part of the reading public is shared by G. R. Shipman, author of the second popularization of technical linguistics, who begins his argument:

> Of all the stock characters in science fiction that I wish the BEM's would eat alive, number one on my list is the Telepathic Martian.
> You know the one I mean. His spaceship lands in an Iowa cornfield . . . the nation panics; . . . the hatches of the spaceship open and the Martian emerges to tell us he wishes us well and only wants to save our civilization from self-destruction.
> In American English, no less. . . .[8]

Most writers of science fiction, Shipman says, who have given up writing about BEM's (Bug-Eyed Monsters, as called in the trade) and turned to weightier matters, use the device of the telepathic Martian in order to avoid the real issue of explaining exactly how two different species can learn to communicate:

> The fact is, most science-fiction writers don't know such techniques exist. . . . In this century descriptive linguistics has made such strides that we can already crack the code of extra-terrestrial speech; yet the average intelligent reader has barely heard of the science. . . . They still refer to the study of language as "philology," and have a vague idea that philologists look for "roots" the way a pig looks for truffles. Well, calling the modern science of linguistics "philology" is like calling atomic physics "natural philosophy"--a subject my grandmother studied, without apparatus, when she was a student at a "female seminary."[9]

---

[8] G. R. Shipman, "How to Talk to a Martian," Astounding Science Fiction, LII (October, 1953), 112.

[9] Ibid., p. 113.

Shipman's style is more formal than Hockett's, but the ultimate issue is the same. Shipman takes a less speculative view, however, throughout saying "when," instead of "if," the time comes to establish communication links with Outsiders, "the linguistic anthropologists will be the ones who forge the link."[10]

It has been proposed, and possibly proved, that some of the linguistic theories and speculations and hypotheses that have appeared as a result of this study will someday be valuable. Even if man never encounters extra-terrestrial beings and never has to communicate with a non-human species, perhaps science fiction-fantasy can still have served the purpose of acquainting readers with their own language and the many varied ways in which we "terrans" have organized our systems of communication. Dr. Hockett was sceptical of this study, with reason, but he expressed a sentiment which has proved to be true. He said in his letter of February 7, 1971:

> Notwithstanding all of which, a study of linguistic knowledge and nonsense in science fiction would be a lot of fun, and I hope you carry through on it.

---

[10]Ibid.

SELECTED BIBLIOGRAPHY

A. Primary Works

Asimov, Isaac. "What Is This Thing Called Love?" <u>Science Fiction Oddities</u>. Edited by Griff Conklin. A Berkley Medallion Book. New York: Berkley Publishing Corporation, 1966.

Boucher, Anthony [Willian Anthony Parker White.] "Barrier," <u>Spectrum IV</u>. Edited by Kingley Amis and Robert Conquest. New York: Doubleday and Company, 1959.

Burgess, Anthony. <u>A Clockwork Orange</u>. The Norton Library. New York: W. W. Norton and Company, Inc., 1963.

De Camp, Lyon Sprague. "New Arcadia." <u>A Gun for Dinosaur and Other Imaginative Tales</u>. Garden City, New York: Doubleday and Company, 1963.

_____. "Wheels of If." <u>Wheels of If and Other Science Fiction</u>. New York: Shasta Publishers, Inc., 1948.

Graves, Robert. <u>Watch the Northwind Rise</u>. An Avon Book. New York: Ferrar, Straus and Cudahy, Inc., 1949. (English title: <u>Seven Days in New Crete</u>.)

Heinlein, Robert. <u>Stranger in a Strange Land</u>. A Berkley Medallion Book. New York: Berkley Publishing Corporation, 1961.

Lafferty, R. A. "What's The Name of That Town?" <u>Science Fiction Oddities</u>. Edited by Griff Conklin. A Berkley Medallion Book. New York: Berkley Publishing Corporation, 1966.

Lewis, Clive Staples. <u>Out of the Silent Planet</u>. New York: Macmillan and Company, 1938.

Miller, Walter M., Jr. <u>A Canticle for Leibowitz</u>. A Bantam Book. New York: J. B. Lippincott Company, 1959.

Nathan, Robert. "A Pride of Carrots." <u>Science Fiction Oddities</u>. Edited by Griff Conklin. A Berkley Medallion Book. New York: Berkley Publishing Corporation, 1966.

Orwell, George [Eric Blair.] *1984*. A Signet Classic. New York: Harcourt, Brace and Company, 1949.

Rand, Ayn. *Anthem*. A Signet Book. New York: The New American Library, 1946.

Tolkien, J. R. R. *The Return of the King*. A Ballentine Book. New York: Ballentine Books, Inc., 1965.

Vance, Jack. *The Languages of Pao*. An Ace Book. New York: Ace Books, Inc., 1958.

Wright, Austin Tappan. *Islandia*. New York: Ferrar and Rinehart, Inc., 1942.

Zamiatin, Eugene. *We*. New York: E. P. Dutton and Company, 1924.

B. Reference

Aiken, Janet R. "English as the International Language." *American Speech*, IX (April, 1934), 98-110.

Amis, Kingsley. *New Maps of Hell*. New York: Harcourt, Brace and Company, 1960.

Black, Max. "Linguistic Relativity: Ideas of Benjamin Lee Whorf." *Philological Review*, LXXVIII (1963), 228-38.

Branden, Nathaniel. *Who Is Ayn Rand?* New York: Random House, Inc., 1962.

Brown, Donna Worrall. "Does Language Structure Influence Thought? Comments on the Psycho-Linguistic Experiment at Michigan." *ETC.: A Review of General Semantics*, XVII (Spring, 1960), 330-345.

Bryant, Margaret. *Modern English and Its Heritage*, 2nd ed. New York: The Macmillan Company, 1962.

Buchanan, Cynthia D. *A Programed Introduction to Linguistics*. Boston: D. C. Heath and Company, 1963.

Burgess, Anthony [John Anthony Burgess Wilson.] "The Electric Grape." *The American Scholar*, XXXV (Autumn, 1966), 720.

---------. *The Novel Now: A Guide to Contemporary Fiction*. New York: W. W. Norton and Company, Inc., 1967.

_____. Urgent Copy: Literary Studies. New York: Norton and Company, Inc., 1968.

Carter, Lin. Tolkien: A Look Behind "The Lord of the Rings." A Ballentine Book. New York: Ballentine Books, Inc., 1969.

Casagrande, Joseph B. "The Ends of Translation." International Journal of American Linguistics, XX (1954), 335-340.

Clarke, Arthur C., editor. Time Probe: The Sciences in Science Fiction. A Dell Book. New York: Dell Publishing Company, 1967.

Cox, Jeff. "Tolkien: The Man Who Invented Nine Languages." Quinto Lingo, (August-September, 1969), 8-11.

Foley, Joseph, and Ayer, James. "Orwell in English and Newspeak: A Computer Translation." College Composition and Communication, XVII (February, 1966), 17-18.

Friend, Joseph H. The Development of American Lexicography. The Hague, Netherlands: Manton and Company, Printers, 1967.

Gaddis, Vincent H. "The New Science of Space Speech." Worlds of Tomorrow, I (1963), 115-123.

Gleason, H. A. An Introduction to Descriptive Linguistics. Revised Edition. New York: Holt, Rinehart and Winston, 1961.

Glenn, Edmund S. "Semantic Difficulties in International Communication." The Use and Misuse of Language. Edited by S. I. Hayakawa. Greenwich, Connecticut: Fawcett Publications, Inc., 1966.

Hall, Robert A., Jr. Hands Off Pidgin English! Garden City, New York: Doubleday and Company, 1955.

_____. Linguistics and Your Language. An Anchor Book. Garden City, New York: Doubleday and Company, Inc., 1960.

_____. Pidgin and Creole Languages. Ithaca, New York: Cornell University Press, 1966.

Hass, Mary R. "Interlingual Word Taboos." American Anthropologist, LIII (July-September, 1951), 338-344.

Hayakawa, S. I. Language in Thought and Action. New York: Harcourt, Brace and Company, 1949.

_____, editor. The Use and Misuse of Language. A Premier Book. Greenwich, Connecticut: Fawcett Publications, Inc., 1966.

Herskovits, Melville J. Cultural Anthropology. New York: Alfred A. Knopf, Inc., 1955.

Hockett, Charles F. "Chinese Versus English: An Exploration of the Whorfian Theses (II)". Language and Culture: A Reader. Edited by Patrick Gleeson and Nancy Wakefield. Columbus, Ohio: Charles E. Merrill Publishing Company, 1968.

_____. A Course in Modern Linguistics. New York: Macmillan and Company, 1958.

_____. "How To Learn Martian." Astounding Science-Fiction, LV (May, 1955), 97-106. In 1960, this magazine changed its name to Analog: Science Fact and Science Fiction.

Hoijer, Harry. "Language and Writing." Man, Culture and Society. Edited by Harry L. Shapiro. New York: Oxford University Press, 1956.

Isaacs, Neil D., and Zimbardo, Rose A., editors. Tolkien and the Critics: Essays on J. R. R. Tolkien's "Lord of the Rings". London: University of Notre Dame Press, 1968.

Jacob, H. A Planned Auxiliary Language. London: Dennis Dobson, Ltd., 1957.

Keesing, Felix M. Cultural Anthropology: The Science of Custom. New York: Holt, Rinehart and Winston, 1962.

Leinster, Colin. "Experiments in Geology -- and Telepathy." Life, LXX (February 26, 1971), 28-29.

Lewis, C. S. Of Other Worlds. New York: Harcourt, Brace and World, Inc., 1966.

Lowie, Robert. The History of Ethnological Theory. New York: Holt, Rinehart and Winston, 1937.

Martinet, Andre. "Structural Linguistics." Anthropology Today. Edited by A. L. Kroeber. Chicago: University of Chicago Press, 1953.

McNelly, Willis E. "Linguistic Relativity in Middle High Martian." The CEA Critic, XXX (March, 1968), 4-5.

Nida, Eugene. *Learning a Foreign Language: A Handbook for Missionaries*. New York: National Council of Churches of Christ in the U.S.A., 1950.

Ornstein, Jacob, and Gage, William W. *The ABC's of Languages and Linguistics*. New York: Chilton Publishers, 1964.

Pei, Mario. "Ending the Language Traffic Jam." *Saturday Review*, XLIX (September 9, 1961), 14-16, 51.

_____. "Language's Curious Couples." *Saturday Review*, XLIII (December 3, 1960), 20-21.

_____. "A Loss for Words." *Saturday Review*, XLVII (November 14, 1964), 82-84.

_____. *One Language for the World: And How to Achieve It*. New York: The Devin-Adair Company, 1961.

Plank, Robert. "Communication in Science Fiction." *The Use and Misuse of Language*. Edited by S. I. Hayakawa. Greenwich, Connecticut: Fawcett Publications, Inc., 1962.

"Publishing Scene." *Saturday Review*, XXX (March 18, 1967), 26.

Pyles, Thomas. "Dictionaries and Usage." *Linguistics Today*. Edited by Archibald A. Hill. New York: Basic Books, Inc., 1969.

Rapoport, Anatole. "What Is Semantics?" *The Use and Misuse of Language*. Edited by S. I. Hayakawa. Greenwich, Connecticut: Fawcett Publications, Inc., 1966.

Richards, I. A. *So Much Nearer: Essays Toward a World English*. 2nd edition. New York: Harcourt, Brace and World, Inc., 1968.

Ross, Alan S. C. "U and Non-U: An Essay in Sociological Linguistics." *The Importance of Language*. Edited by Max Black. Englewood Cliffs, New Jersey: Prentice-Hall, Inc., 1962.

Shipman, G. R. "How to Talk to a Martian." *Astounding Science Fiction*, LII (October, 1953), 112-120.

Stern, Theodore. "Drum and Whistle 'Languages': An Analysis of Speech Surrogates." *American Anthropologist*, LIX (June, 1957), 487-506.

Sykes, Christopher. "What U-Future." *Noblesse Oblige*. Edited by Nancy Mitford. New York: Harper and Brothers, Inc., 1956.

Tinker, John. "Old English in Rohan." *Tolkien and the Critics*. Edited by Neil D. Isaacs and Rose A Zimbardo. London: University of Notre Dame Press, 1968.

Tolkien, J.R.R. "On Fairy Stories." *The Tolkien Reader*. A Ballentine Book. New York: Ballentine Books, Inc., 1966.

_____. *Poems and Songs of Middle Earth*. New York: Caedmon TC 1231, 1967.

Vonnegut, Kurt, Jr. "The Dictionary." *Welcome to The Monkey House*. A Dell Book. New York: Dell Publishing Company, Inc., 1968.

Walsh, Chad. *From Utopia to Nightmare*. New York: Harper and Row, Publishers, 1962.

Weekley, Ernest. "On Dictionaries." *Dictionaries and That Dictionary*. Edited by James H. Sledd and Wilma R. Ebbitt. Chicago: Scott, Foresman and Company, 1962.

Whorf, Benjamin Lee. "An American Indian Model of the Universe." *Language and Culture: A Reader*. Edited by Patrick Gleeson and Nancy Wakefield. Columbus, Ohio: Charles E. Merrill Publishing Company, 1968.

_____. "Science and Linguistics." *Language and Culture: A Reader*. Edited by Patrick Gleeson and Nancy Wakefield. Columbus, Ohio: Charles E. Merrill Publishing Company, 1968.

C. Special Reference: Science Fiction

In this section and the next, I have chosen to include additional items, even though some lack complete bibliographic information.

"Annotated Checklist of Secondary Articles Relating to Science Fiction." *Extrapolation: Newsletter of the SF Section of Modern Language Association*, XI (May, 1970); XII (December, 1970); XII (May, 1971).

Amis, Kingsley. *New Maps of Hell*. New York: Harcourt, Brace and Company, 1960.

_____. Starting Points.

Aring, Charles D. "The Case Becomes Less Strange." American Scholar, XXX (1960-61), 67-78.

Asimov, Isaac. Social Science Fiction.

Bailey, J. O. Pilgrims Through Space and Time: Trends and Patterns in Scientific and Utopian Fiction. Los Angeles, California: Argus Publishing Corporation, 1947.

Bernabeu, E. P. "Science Fiction: A New Mythos." The Psychoanalytic Quarterly, XXVI (1957), 4, 527-535.

Bleiler, Everett F. Checklist of Fantastic Literature. Chicago, 1948.

Bretnor, Reginald, editor. Modern Science Fiction, Its Meaning and Its Future. New York: Coward-McCann, Inc., 1953.

Clarke, Ignatius F. The Tale of the Future, from the Beginning to the Present Day. London, 1961.

Crawford, Joseph H., et al. '333': A Bibliography of the Science Fantasy Novel. Providence, Rhode Island, 1953.

Davenport, Basil. An Inquiry into Science Fiction. New York: Longmans, Green and Company, 1955.

Day, Bradford M. Supplemental Checklist of Fantastic Literature. Denver, 1963.

Day, Donald B., editor. Index to the SF Magazines 1926-1950. New York: Perri Press, 1952.

De Camp, L. Sprague. Lands Beyond. New York: Rinehard, Holt and Winston, 1952.

_____. "Language for Time Travellers." Astounding Science Fiction, (July, 1938). Also reprinted in Coming Attractions, Martin Greenberg, editor. New York: Gnome Press, 1957.

_____. Science Fiction Handbook. New York: Hermitage Press, 1953.

Derleth, August. Beyond Space and Time. New York, 1950.

Elliot, Robert C. "The Fear of Utopia." Centennial Review, VII (1963), 237-251.

Franklin, H. Bruce. "Fictions of Science." TLS, (October 25, 1963), 865.

Gerber, Richard. Utopian Fantasy: A Study of Utopian Fiction Since the End of the Nineteenth Century. New York: Hillary House, Inc., 1956.

Green, Roger Lancelyn. Into Other Worlds. London, 1957.

Heard, Gerald. Science Fiction, Morals, and Religion.

Hillegas, Mark Robert. "Dystopian Science Fiction: New Index to the Human Situation." New Mexico Quarterly, XXXI (1961), 238-249.

_____. The Future as Nightmare: H. G. Wells and the Anti-Utopians. New York: Oxford University Press, 1967.

Hockett, Charles F. "How to Learn Martian." Astounding Science Fiction, LV (May, 1955), 97-106. Also reprinted in Coming Attractions, Martin Greenberg, editor. New York: Gnome Press, 1957.

Knight, Damon. In Search of Wonder. Chicago: Advent Publishers, 1956.

Koestler, Arthur. The Boredom of Fantasy.

_____. The Ghost in the Machine. New York, 1968.

Kornbluth, Cyril, et al. The Science Fiction Novel. Chicago: Advent Publishers, 1959.

Krueger, John R. "Names and Nomenclatures in Science Fiction." Names, XIV (December, 1966), 203-214.

Lewis, C. S. An Experiment in Criticism. New York: Cambridge University Press, 1961.

Manuel, Frank, editor. Utopias and Utopian Thought. Boston, 1966.

Meyer, Karl E. The New America: The Age of the Smooth Deal. New York: Basic Books, Inc., 1961.

MIT SF Society. Index to the SF Magazines 1966-1970. Cambridge, Mass.: MIT SF Society, 1971.

Moskowitz, Samuel. Explorers of the Infinite. New York: World Publishing Co., 1963. This is a collection of bibliographic biographies of leading writers of science fiction.

———. *Seekers of Tomorrow: Masters of Science Fiction.* Cleveland, Ohio: World Publishing Company, 1966.

Philmus, Robert M. *Into the Unknown: The Evolution of Science Fiction from Francis Godwin to H. G. Wells.* Berkley: University of California Press, 1970.

Plank, Robert. "Communication in Science Fiction." *The Use and Misuse of Language.* Edited by S. I. Hayakawa. Greenwich, Connecticut: Fawcett Publications, Inc., 1962.

———. "The Golem and the Robot." *Literature and Psychology,* XV (1965), 12-28.

———. "Names and Roles of Characters in Science Fiction." *Names,* IX (1961), 151-159.

———. "The Reproduction of Psychosis in Science Fiction." *International Record of Medicine,* CLXVII (1954), 7, 407-421.

Schwonke, Martin. *Vom Staatsroman zur Science Fiction.* Stuttgart, 1957.

Shipman, G. R. "How to Talk to a Martian." *Astounding Science Fiction,* LII (October, 1953), 112-120. Also reprinted in *Coming Attractions,* Martin Greenberg, ed. New York: Gnome Press, 1957.

Sisk, John P. *The Future of Prediction.*

Sontag, Susan. *The Imagination of Disaster.*

Strauss, Erwin, editor. *Index to the SF Magazines 1951-1965.* Cambridge, Mass.: MIT SF Society, 1966.

Tuck, Donald H. *A Handbook of Science Fiction and Fantasy.* Hobart, Tasmania: (Published by the author), 1959.

Walsh, Chad. *From Utopia to Nightmare.* New York: Harper and Row, Publishers, 1962.

Woodcock, George. "Utopias in Negative," *Sewanee Review,* LXIV (1956), 81-97.

Yershov, P. *Science Fiction and Utopian Fantasy in Soviet Literature.* New York: Research Program in the U.S.S.R., 1954.

D. Additional Reading

Burgess, Anthony. *The Doctor is Sick.* New York: Heinemann Publishing Company, 1960.

Burroughs, Edgar Rice. *Escape on Venus.*

Cortezar, Julio. "8 Times 8 Equals Gliglish." *Hopscotch.* New York: Pantheon Publications, 1966.

De Camp, L. Sprague. *The Continent Makers.* New York: Doubleday, Doran and Company, 1954.

Delaney, Samuel. *Babel 17.* An Ace Book. New York: Ace Books, Inc., 1968.

Kornbluth, Cyril, and Poul, Frederick. *The Space Merchants.* 1953.

Maine, Charles Eric. *He Owned the World.*

McAllister, Bruce. "The Faces Outside." *9th Annual Edition of the Year's Best Science Fiction.* Edited by Judith Merrill. A Dell Book. New York: Dell Publishing Company, Inc., 1964.

Smith, Cordwainer. "Drunkboat." *9th Annual Edition of the Year's Best Science Fiction.* A Dell Book. Edited by Judith Merrill. New York: Dell Publishing Company, Inc., 1964.

Updike, John. "In Praise of $(C_{10}H_9O_5)^x$." (A poem) *Telephone Poles.* New York: Alfred A. Knopf, 1963.

Vonnegut, Kurt, Jr. "2BR2B." *Worlds of If,* XII (January, 1962), 59ff. Also reprinted in *Best Science Fiction from "Worlds of If",* (1964).

APPENDIX: BIOGRAPHICAL DATA

Amis, Kingsley (1922-   ) Born in England, Amis earned his
  B.A. at Oxford University (first class honors in English)
  and also did graduate work there. As a lecturer in English at Cambridge University, he also lectured abroad,
  and was a visiting lecturer at Princeton University 1958-
  59. As a literary critic, he collaborated with R. P.
  Blackmur in courses in creative writing; claiming that
  utopias and dystopias are the new "heavens and hells"
  of science fiction, his New Maps of Hell: A Survey of
  Science Fiction is basically a collection of his lectures
  delivered at Princeton. Amis is also a motion picture
  reviewer for Esquire, contributor to both popular and
  scholarly periodicals, author of social satires (his
  Lucky Jim, 1954, was made into a movie in 1957), and is
  considered by some critics to be one of the "young
  angries" of English writers.

Asimov, Isaac (1920-   ) Born in Russia, Asimov received his
  education in the United States; his highest degree is a
  Ph.D. in chemistry from Columbia University, received in
  1948, but he has done post-doctoral work in several fields
  of science. He has written biochemistry textbooks for
  medical students, and his scientific writings now number
  almost sixty books and hundreds of articles, in subjects
  such as mathematics, chemistry, linguistics, astronomy,
  biology, biochemistry, physiology, and history. As a
  writer of science fiction, he is probably best known for
  his Three Laws of Robotics and his Toynbeean studies of
  the rise and fall of galactic civilizations, although his
  total output reaches almost astronomical proportions.
  Asimov taught at Boston University School of Medicine
  until 1958, when he decided to devote full time to writing.
  He is intensely interested in almost everything, and was
  a member of the usage panel, organized in 1965, of the
  American Heritage Dictionary of the English Language.
  Asimov also writes a monthly column in Fantasy and Science
  Fiction, which recently devoted an entire issue (October,
  1966) to him.

Boucher, Anthony [William Anthony Parker White] (1911-1968)
  Boucher began his writing career with mystery stories,
  but also wrote radio and television shows, translated
  from Spanish and French and Portuguese, was a regular
  book reviewer for the New York Times and the New York

Herald Tribune, and was a avid opera enthusiast. He held a B.A. from the University of Southern California, 1932, and a M.A. from Berkley, 1934, both degrees in drama, although he originally intended to be a teacher of languages. Until his death, he wrote a review of the year's best science fiction, published as a regular feature in the <u>Annual Edition of the Year's Best S-F</u>, edited by Judith Merril. Boucher was one of the earliest enthusiasts of science fiction as a literary genre and was particularly annoyed by "people who say they never read science fiction but who think <u>1984</u> and <u>Brave New World</u> are wonderful." Boucher said he had lost count of the number of short stories and novelettes he wrote.

Burgess, Anthony [John Anthony Burgess Wilson] (1917-   )
Born in Manchester, England, Burgess received his B.A. (with honors) from Manchester University in 1940. He has lectured in phonetics and linguistics, music and literature, published scholarly articles in England, America, and Japan. His non-fiction writings include a text book on literature (1958), <u>Language Made Plain</u> (1964), and <u>Re Joyce</u> (1965), a study of James Joyce. Between the years 1956 and 1967, Burgess produced seventeen major novels, claiming to have used several pseudomyns so that his tremendous output would not be so apparent. Critics observe that he exploits words in much the same way a poet does, and a great portion of his novels demonstrate his fascination with language.

De Camp, Lyon Sprague (1907-   ) Born in New York City, de Camp now lives in Ithaca, New York. He is a man of versatile and varied interests, having written (with his wife Catherine de Camp) many non-fiction works on history and archeology whose fictional and hypothetic counterparts appear in his science fiction stories. His articles on phonetics have appeared in scholarly journals since the 1930's, and he is also author of one hundred fifty other technical articles, over one hundred short stories, seventy-six radio scripts for Voice of America, and two non-fiction reference books dealing with science fiction as a genre. He is a member of the History of Science Society, Association Phonetique Internationale, Authors Club of New York, and others, and recipient of several book awards. He received his B.S. degree from California Institute of Technology in 1930, attended MIT, and received his M.S. at Stevens Institute of Technology in 1933. His special interests are travel (he was once a uranium prospector), gardening, language study.

Graves, Robert von Ranke (1895-   ) London-born Graves, one
of ten children, attended six preparatory schools before
entering the Charterhouse in 1914. He enjoyed boxing
and mountain-climbing, as well as literary studies, and
he began his literary career as a poet. After many years
of poverty, with his wife and four children, he completed
his degree at Oxford in 1926, and became professor of
English at the University of Cairo. He was friends with
T. E. Lawrence ("Lawrence of Arabia"), and in addition to
his biography on Lawrence and his two autobiographies, he
became a noted novelist with I, Claudius in 1934. Many
of his works deal with reconstructions of Roman life,
and has collaborated with many modern authors, among
them John Crowe Ransom, E. E. Cummings, and T. S. Eliot.

Heinlein, Robert Anson (1907-   ) Born in Missouri, Heinlein
is a graduate of the U. S. Naval Academy (1929) and did
graduate work at UCLA. He is a member of many organiza-
tions, among them the American Institute of Astronautics
and Aeronautics, Authors League of America, and American
Association for the Advancement of Science. Since he
began writing science fiction stories in 1939, he has
written more than one hundred fifty novels and novelettes,
and he received five awards for the best science fiction
of the year. Critics claim that Heinlein's books are
heavily didactic.

Huxley, Aldous Leonard (1894-1963) Grandson of Thomas H.
Huxley, grand-nephew of Matthew Arnold, and brother of
Julian Huxley, Aldous contracted keratitis and was almost
completely blind when he was eighteen. His first novel
was written in Braille. Because a career in biology was
impossible, he entered Oxford University as a reader in
English literature and philology, earning his degree in
1915. His writing career continued in India, Italy, and
France, until he heard, in 1938, of the Bates method of
eye-training, and moved to California to undergo treatment. Although the treatment helped, and he was able to
write, most of his famous novels and essays were written
before this period (Crome Yellow in 1921, Point Counter
Point in 1928, Brave New World in 1932). His last book
was Island (1962), a utopian counterpart to Brave New
World. Critics describe his books as "a too bright
picture of a society in decadence" and claim that his
real genius was as an essayist, not a novelist.

Lewis, Clive Staples (1898-1963) Born in Ireland, Lewis was
educated privately until he entered University College,
Oxford, where he became a lecturer in 1924. A personal
friend of J. R. R. Tolkien, the two men were part of an
informal group calling themselves the Inklings; it was

Lewis who urged Tolkien to publish The Hobbit and Tolkien who urged Lewis to write his trilogy. Lewis is known as a scholar of medieval literature (The Allegory of Love in 1936, plus others), and received wide acclaim for his satirical The Screwtape Letters in 1942. Lewis, who never married, claimed that his Christianity was philosophical, not emotional, and most of his fiction writings are religious in nature. Among his writings is a series of children's books, the Narnia stories.

Miller, Walter M., Jr. (1923-   ) Educated as an electrical engineer, Miller spent four years in the Air Force, and he began writing in 1949, when he was in a plaster cast. He has written dozens of radio shows, many science fiction stories, and one novel. Miller now lives in Florida with his wife and children.

Orwell, George [Eric Blair] (1903-1950) Born in Motihari, Bengal, Orwell received his education at Eton, 1917-1921. Orwell was primarily a political writer, and in addition to writing, almost made a career of serving in foreign political wars. He claimed to detest London, where he lived many years, was always in poor health, and consciously avoided associating himself with any political party. In his latter years, Orwell was especially concerned with corruption of the English language as a factor in political freedom, and, in addition to his essays on the subject, intended 1984 as an illustration of how such a process could be successful.

Rand, Ayn [Mrs. Frank O'Connor] (1905-   ) Ayn Rand was born in Petrograd, Russia, where she spent most of her childhood. Biographical information is always sketchy, inasmuch as Miss Rand is rather secretive about her personal life. She left home early, after her family had moved to America, and worked at many jobs before publishers began to accept her writings. The Fountainhead (1943) was rejected by twelve publishers at first, and she claims that all of her personality and philosophy is embodied in this book. She is violently anti-collectivism, and her ego-centered philosophy, called "Objectivism," is the theme of The Objectivist Newsletter, a periodical she co-edits with Nathaniel Branden, published in California. Her philosophy is currently embodied by several "cults" in California, and she occasionally appears on television shows to talk about her views.

Tolkien, John Ronald Reuel (1892-1973?) Born in South Africa and orphaned at the age of twelve, Tolkien and his brother were raised by a Roman Catholic priest in England. His highest degree is an M.A. in English language, earned at the University of Leeds in 1919, but other than many honorary degrees presented to him, he has never earned the Ph.D. Nevertheless, he is recognized as an authority on Old and Middle English and is well known for his scholarly work on Beowulf and Chaucer. As a young man, even before he worked on the <u>Oxford English Dictionary</u>, he amused himself by inventing make-believe languages, and <u>The Lord of the Rings</u> was made to provide a world for them, rather than vice versa. A life-long friend of the late C. S. Lewis, Tolkien retired from his position in Oxford University in 1959 and now resides in Headington, with his wife, where he is in virtual seclusion working on a sequel to <u>The Lord of the Rings</u>, to be called <u>The Silmarillion</u>. Sprague de Camp, who recently visited the Tolkiens, describes him as "hale and hearty, as alert and keen-witted as ever, a little above average height, although heavy-set and stooped . . . outspoken, even argumentative," Tolkien is reportedly annoyed by studies of his work ("while I am alive, anyway") and the contents of <u>The Silmarillion</u>, under composition for more than ten years now, is still a mystery.

Vance, Jack (1918-   ) A native Californian, Vance studied physics and journalism at the University of California, served in World War II, and is now a free-lance writer. He describes himself as a "professional word-mechanic," but Arthur C. Clarke calls him "one of the heirs to the mantle of Professor J. R. R. Tolkien." Vance, well noted in the field of science fiction, is particulary interested in media of communication--language, colors, masks, music-- and is perhaps best known for his novel <u>The Dragon Masters</u>.

Wright, Austin Tappan (c. 1880-1934) Wright was a lawyer, never an author. <u>Islandia</u> is the title given by his wife and daughter to the book when they offered it for publication after his death in 1934 in an automobile crash. Wright wrote the adventures of John Lang, his hero, as a personal hobby and, probably, as his private utopia. The hand-written manuscript was more than 2200 pages long, including mythology and history and geneological tables, plus other material relating to his land of Islandia-- all of which his family deleted before publication. The book, published in 1942, contains only 1,018 pages.

Zamiatin, Eugene (c. 1875-1937) As a young man, Zamiatin was several times imprisoned for his revolutionary work during Tsarist days in Russia, and he lectured after the revolution on behalf of Lenin and was rewarded with a government position. However, his anxiety toward growing totalitarianism caused him to write We, in 1920, as a warning. The manuscript, not publishable in Russia, was smuggled into the United States and published in 1924. As a consequence, Russian authorities banned the sale of his other books and refused to publish any future writings; Stalin granted Zamiatin's request to leave Russia, and he exiled himself in Paris, never writing anything of importance until his death in 1937.

SCIENCE FICTION

An Arno Press Collection

FICTION

About, Edmond. **The Man with the Broken Ear.** 1872
Allen, Grant. **The British Barbarians:** A Hill-Top Novel. 1895
Arnold, Edwin L. **Lieut. Gullivar Jones:** His Vacation. 1905
Ash, Fenton. **A Trip to Mars.** 1909
Aubrey, Frank. **A Queen of Atlantis.** 1899
Bargone, Charles (Claude Farrere, pseud.). **Useless Hands.** [1926]
Beale, Charles Willing. **The Secret of the Earth.** 1899
Bell, Eric Temple (John Taine, pseud.). **Before the Dawn.** 1934
Benson, Robert Hugh. **Lord of the World.** 1908
Beresford, J. D. **The Hampdenshire Wonder.** 1911
Bradshaw, William R. **The Goddess of Atvatabar.** 1892
Capek, Karel. **Krakatit.** 1925
Chambers, Robert W. **The Gay Rebellion.** 1913
Colomb, P. et al. **The Great War of 189—.** 1893
Cook, William Wallace. **Adrift in the Unknown.** n.d.
Cummings, Ray. **The Man Who Mastered Time.** 1929
[DeMille, James]. **A Strange Manuscript Found in a Copper Cylinder.** 1888
Dixon, Thomas. **The Fall of a Nation:** A Sequel to the Birth of a Nation. 1916
England, George Allan. **The Golden Blight.** 1916
Fawcett, E. Douglas. **Hartmann the Anarchist.** 1893
Flammarion, Camille. **Omega:** The Last Days of the World. 1894
Grant, Robert et al. **The King's Men:** A Tale of To-Morrow. 1884
Grautoff, Ferdinand Heinrich (Parabellum, pseud.). **Banzai!** 1909
Graves, C. L. and E. V. Lucas. **The War of the Wenuses.** 1898
Greer, Tom. **A Modern Daedalus.** [1887]

Griffith, George. **A Honeymoon in Space.** 1901

Grousset, Paschal (A. Laurie, pseud.). **The Conquest of the Moon.** 1894

Haggard, H. Rider. **When the World Shook.** 1919

Hernaman-Johnson, F. **The Polyphemes.** 1906

Hyne, C. J. Cutcliffe. **Empire of the World.** [1910]

In The Future. [1875]

Jane, Fred T. **The Violet Flame.** 1899

Jefferies, Richard. **After London; Or, Wild England.** 1885

Le Queux, William. **The Great White Queen.** [1896]

London, Jack. **The Scarlet Plague.** 1915

Mitchell, John Ames. **Drowsy.** 1917

Morris, Ralph. **The Life and Astonishing Adventures of John Daniel.** 1751

Newcomb, Simon. **His Wisdom The Defender:** A Story. 1900

Paine, Albert Bigelow. **The Great White Way.** 1901

Pendray, Edward (Gawain Edwards, pseud.). **The Earth-Tube.** 1929

Reginald, R. and Douglas Menville. **Ancestral Voices:** An Anthology of Early Science Fiction. 1974

Russell, W. Clark. **The Frozen Pirate.** 2 vols. in 1. 1887

Shiel, M. P. **The Lord of the Sea.** 1901

Symmes, John Cleaves (Captain Adam Seaborn, pseud.). **Symzonia.** 1820

Train, Arthur and Robert W. Wood. **The Man Who Rocked the Earth.** 1915

Waterloo, Stanley. **The Story of Ab:** A Tale of the Time of the Cave Man. 1903

White, Stewart E. and Samuel H. Adams. **The Mystery.** 1907

Wicks, Mark. **To Mars Via the Moon.** 1911

Wright, Sydney Fowler. **Deluge: A Romance** and **Dawn.** 2 vols. in 1. 1928/1929

SCIENCE FICTION

NON-FICTION:
Including Bibliographies,
Checklists and Literary Criticism

Aldiss, Brian and Harry Harrison. **SF Horizons.** 2 vols. in 1. 1964/1965

Amis, Kingsley. **New Maps of Hell.** 1960

Barnes, Myra. **Linguistics and Languages in Science Fiction-Fantasy.** 1974

Cockcroft, T. G. L. **Index to the Weird Fiction Magazines.** 2 vols. in 1 1962/1964

Cole, W. R. **A Checklist of Science-Fiction Anthologies.** 1964

Crawford, Joseph H. et al. **"333": A Bibliography of the Science-Fantasy Novel.** 1953

Day, Bradford M. **The Checklist of Fantastic Literature in Paperbound Books.** 1965

Day, Bradford M. **The Supplemental Checklist of Fantastic Literature.** 1963

Gove, Philip Babcock. **The Imaginary Voyage in Prose Fiction.** 1941

Green, Roger Lancelyn. **Into Other Worlds:** Space-Flight in Fiction, From Lucian to Lewis. 1958

Menville, Douglas. **A Historical and Critical Survey of the Science Fiction Film.** 1974

Reginald, R. **Contemporary Science Fiction Authors,** First Edition. 1970

Samuelson, David. **Visions of Tomorow:** Six Journeys from Outer to Inner Space. 1974